Traveling in Place

A History of
Armchair Travel

Traveling
in Place

BERND
STIEGLER

*Translated from the German
by Peter Filkins*

*The University of Chicago Press
Chicago and London*

Bernd Stiegler is professor of twentieth-century German literature and of literature and the media at the University of Konstanz.

Peter Filkins is a poet and teaches literature at Bard College.

Originally published as *Reisender Stillstand*
© 2010 by S. Fischer Verlag GmbH, Frankfurt am Main
All rights reserved by S. Fischer Verlag GmbH, Frankfurt am Main.

The University of Chicago Press, Chicago 60637
The University of Chicago Press, Ltd., London
English translation © 2013 by The University of Chicago
All rights reserved. Published 2013.
Printed in the United States of America

The translation of this work was funded by Geisteswissenschaften International — Translation Funding for the Humanities and Social Sciences from Germany, a joint initiative of the Fritz Thyssen Foundation, the German Federal Foreign Office, the collecting society VG WORT, and the Börsenverein des Deutschen Buchhandels (German Publishers & Booksellers Association).

22 21 20 19 18 17 16 15 14 13 1 2 3 4 5
ISBN-13: 978-0-226-77467-1 (cloth)
ISBN-13: 978-0-226-08115-1 (e-book)
DOI: 10.7208/chicago/9780226081151.001.0001

Library of Congress Cataloging-in-Publication Data

Stiegler, Bernd.
    [Reisender Stillstand. English]
    Traveling in place : a history of armchair travel / Bernd Stiegler ; translated from the German by Peter Filkins.
        pages ; cm
    Includes bibliographical references and index.
    ISBN 978-0-226-77467-1 (hardcover ; alkaline paper) — ISBN 978-0-226-08115-1 (e-book)   1. Travel in literature.   2. Rooms in literature.   3. European literature — History and criticism.   I. Title.
    PN56.T7S8513 2013
    809'.9332 — dc23
                                                2013011718

⊗ This paper meets the requirements of ANSI/NISO Z39.48-1992 (Permanence of Paper).

For the room traveler Sara
and
the distant traveler Petra

CONTENTS

Brief Travel Guide

Therefore it doesn't matter at all if you travel really far away
into unknown regions. The nature of this kind of travel
occurs within. You stand in a different relation to the external
world. . . . Perhaps you don't even need to leave your room?

Balázs, 94

Even though it may appear so, this is not a book for the homebody,
the agoraphobe, or the reluctant traveler—even though, admittedly, they are frequently the subjects of the following texts. Indeed, this book should not be taken as an introduction to traveling
around one's room, but much more as a history of this special type
of travel: room travel. Traveling in place. Travel into the near distance and the distantly near. Traveling without traveling. Traveling without budging an inch, and yet setting a great deal into motion at the same time. Virtual explorations of the everyday world,
which in the process become pointedly strange. That's what this
book is about.

Just as the room journey represents a kind of experiment—
whereby the traveler distances himself from his usual surroundings without actually leaving them—so this book is an experiment. More to the point, by gathering so many examples of such
journeys from a period that stretches over two centuries, doesn't
such a book then become an exploration of realms of experience

as well? What kind of experience, then, do all these very different journeys have in common? And finally, does the history of room travel also result in a history of realms of experience that have changed as well?

The practice of room travel can perhaps be expressed by a formulation for which I am indebted to Viktor Shklovsky: defamiliarization, *ostranenie*, the "estranging of objects. . . . The purpose . . . is to lead us to a knowledge of a thing through the organ of sight instead of recognition" (Shklovsky 6). This is how he describes the project of art. The same applies to room travel: to estrange ourselves from supposedly familiar spaces, to take them in by observing them closely with the applied eye of an ethnologist in order to explore them as if stepping into them for the very first time, or at a minimum seeing them in a new light.

Yet what is room travel? In 1781, Friedrich Nicolai already posed a question that anticipated the global tourist industry: how is it possible to maintain a sense of home while on a journey? Only a short while later, the question was turned around: how is a journey possible while at home? Xavier de Maistre's *Voyage autour de ma chambre* (*A Journey around My Room*) of 1794 answered this question and at the same time marked a new genre of travel writing. De Maistre used a forty-two-day house arrest to bring an ostensibly long-planned project to fruition—and travel around his room. The result was a brief, ironic, witty, profound, and unintentionally provocative book that even today has hardly lost any of its freshness. It is a unique travel account that is about the near distance and the distantly near, and about what happens inside a room in which nothing really happens at all. Room travel involves a type of *de-tachment*, which involves pulling back from the realm of the habitual to explore and describe it anew.

Room journeys—and this lays down the most important rule of the "legs" of the journey that follow—are not at all imaginary. They set forth no utopias, nor do they have any place that serves

Installé dans ma bibliothèque, j'oublie toutes mes douleurs.

0.0 Frontispiece to S. D'Houay, *Voyage dans ma maison* (Rouen, 1880).

as a final destination, but instead concentrate on each supposedly familiar space here and now. They describe no dream worlds but rather the banal space of the everyday. They don't explore exotic, far-off places, but instead remain in immediate surroundings: in a room, on our own street or in our own town. Yet these spaces can transform themselves whenever the observer begins to travel around them, transforming and turning them into genuine realms of experience that have been previously hidden or consumed by the gray mildew of the everyday. The journey around one's room is an open sesame for the everyday that at once opens something other and makes it accessible.

Xavier de Maistre's journey was in no way to remain the only one of its kind. Down through the years, countless examples of this hardly discussed literary domain have been published. Most of them are not the kind of literature generally thought of as canonical. Many of their authors have been lost to time, and many of the texts are found in dusty volumes or books left unread in large libraries. And yet that doesn't reduce their value at all. What follows is less about the literary meaning and aesthetic caliber of texts often published in far-flung places than about texts as experiments, as explorations and descriptions of realms of experience.

In the following chapters, the spaces through which we travel while journeying through a room will progress in rough chronological order, changing a great deal along the way and altering our relation to the near and the far as well as to objects that surround us, and not least of all to ourselves. To help us to see this is the aim of this unique travel guide. The readings are composed of twenty-one legs, exactly half as many as de Maistre's journey, plus a short excursion devoted to a journey that certainly is a distant one, but which for many room travelers is an important reference point: Jules Verne's *Around the World in 80 Days*. Each leg can be enjoyed independently of the other legs throughout. At the end of each are suggestions for travel reading that might also aid further explorations. "Thus I think," wrote Friedrich David Jaquet, a room traveler at the start of the nineteenth century, "the journey around my room can never bore me, and I am as justified in making it as is Swift in journeying to the moon. And so the other extreme was available, and the journey began" (Jaquet 9). May this also happen for the reader of this book. Indeed, "Raise the anchor! It is time!" (Baudelaire 261).

Travel Reading

Balázs, Béla. "Reisen." In *Ein Baedecker der Seele und andere Feuilletons*. Berlin, 1930. (First published in *Der Phantasie-Reiseführer/Das ist ein Baedecker der Seele/Für Sommerfrischler*. Berlin/Vienna/Leipzig, 1925.)

Baudelaire, Charles. "The Voyage." In *The Flowers of Evil & Paris Spleen*. Trans. William H. Crosby. Brockport, NY, 1991.

Jaquet, Friedrich David. *Reise in meinem Zimmer in den Jahren 1812 und 1813*. Riga, 1813.

Nicolai, Friedrich. *Beschreibung einer Reise durch Deutschland und die Schweiz im Jahre 1781*. 12 vols. Berlin/Stettin, 1783–96.

Piechotta, Hans Joachim. "Erkenntnistheorie Voraussetzungen der Beschreibung: Friedrich Nicholais Reise durch Deutschland und die Schweiz im Jahre 1781." In *Reise und Utopie*. Ed. Ralph-Rainer Wuthenow. Frankfurt am Main, 1976. 98–150.

Shklovsky, Viktor. "Art as Device" [1916]. In *Theory of Prose*. Trans. Benjamin Sher. Elmwood Park, FL, 1990. 1–15.

The Journey around the Room

Look for the secret to happiness nowhere else but within yourself.

> Abbé Gresset, *Vert-Vert* (1733); motto of the first edition of
> de Maistre's *Voyage autour de ma chambre*

How many a man has journeyed forth without leaving
his room.

> Perin, frontispiece

In many a deep author of wisdom quite sublime,
I've read that too much travel is an utter waste of time

> Anonymous reviewer of *Voyage autour de ma chambre*, 977,
> and Jaquet, 43

In the spring of 1790, Xavier de Maistre, brother of the conservative political philosopher Joseph de Maistre, made the best that he could of a house arrest and commenced a forty-two-day journey around his room, which he turned into a detailed travel account that not only would become an exceedingly renowned work of French literature but also launched a literary genre. De Maistre was in no way as travel-shy as it may appear at first glance. He was no homebody, but on the contrary urbane and a proponent of technological innovation. Together with his brother he took a ride in Montgolfière's early hot-air balloon, writing about it in two

7

articles, and during his lifetime traveled a great deal, though often for political reasons.

Even today, his *Voyage autour de ma chambre* (*A Journey around My Room*) is available in many editions and translations, and is a staple of comprehensive high school exams; it is a classic text whose immediate success came as a surprise to its author, yet it pointed the way for many other works to take up the idea and develop it further. Already on February 16, 1803, a vaudeville comedy by René Perin premiered at the Théâtre de l'Ambigu Comique in Paris, which was followed by many more right up until the midnineteenth century, while just a few years after the first edition of de Maistre's book there appeared numerous books and travel accounts in the same vein. Even de Maistre himself was a bit surprised by the success of his book. On December 31, 1799, at the turn of the century, he wrote to his brother Joseph about his colossal success: "I've seen copies of it everywhere. It's been translated into German. There's also another book with the title *Zweite Reise um . . .* (*Second Journey Around . . .*), etc., that's been translated as well. That's wonderful, while a third one along the same lines, *Reise durch meine Taschen* (*Journey through My Pockets*), is mediocre" (de Maistre, *Lettres*, 1:60). Many years later, he would write a kind of sequel, an *Expédition nocturne autour de ma chambre* (*A Nocturnal Expedition around My Room*), about travel which lasted only for a single night. Charles Nodier commented smugly on the success of this new type of travel literature: "For ages nothing but travel books or children's books have been published. Have you read *Voyage autour de ma chambre*, *Le Voyage autour de vingt-quatre heures*, *Le Voyage au Palais-Royal*, *Le Voyage dans le boudoir de Pauline*, *Le Voyage dans mes poches . . .* ? It's a regular mania" (Nodier, in Sangsue, 166).

De Maistre's slim book, *Voyage autour de ma chambre*, which runs to barely a hundred pages, is full of allusions, not only to the tradition of travel writing but also to literature. On the one hand, he ironically distances himself from very well-known travel accounts of his time when implicitly or explicitly quoting them, while on the other he moves toward Laurence Sterne's recent accentuation of the travel account in *A Sentimental Journey*, which is less about stunning discoveries and explorations among foreign peoples, animals, and marvels than about the *sensations* experienced by the traveler himself. Nor is the depiction of these free of irony in his account. Any such discovery — and this is often the case — whether the account is more about the object or the subject, even if it is tinged with irony, is also a discovery about what is being discovered. De Maistre's journey explores the long-familiar world that is seen anew with the gaze brought to it through the distancing perspectives of travel *and* irony.

De Maistre added a foreword to the new edition of 1812 that pointedly addresses the *topos* of journeys of discovery in an ironic manner: "It's in no way our intention to belittle the merits of those travelers who have circled the planet in order to publish their discoveries and interesting adventures. Magellan, Drake, Anson, Cook, etc., were without doubt worthy men. However, it is permissible and, if we are not mistaken, even our duty to suggest that the particular merit of the *Voyage autour de ma chambre* is that this book is superior to all others previous to it. The most illustrious journeys can be repeated: a fine line drawn across all maps shows us the route, and each is free to follow in the footsteps of these clever men who once made the journey themselves. The situation is different with the *Voyage autour de ma chambre*. It occurs only once and no mortal can boast being able to again repeat it, particularly since the world depicted within it no longer exists" (de Maistre, *Nouvelles*, 27). Thus De Maistre emphasizes in ironic fashion that although the routes of the explorers' ships can be repeated, the journey around one's room is, regardless of whether intended so, of a transient nature, necessarily singular and therefore not repeatable. The experiences involved in the journey around one's room are not just attached to the place but also bound to time, being explorations of a space whose aim is to invoke stories and experiences that cannot be repeated. Even if numerous models of de Maistre's room journey can be found right up to the present, the discoveries that each traveler makes are attached to the experience of that particular space. Each room journey discovers realms of experience and makes these the subject of a travel account.

De Maistre's begins in classic manner with an orientation: "My room is, according to the measurement of Fr. Beccaria, situated on the forty-fifth degree of latitude; it stretches from east to west; it forms a long rectangle, thirty-six paces in circumference if you hug the wall. My journey will, however, measure much more than this, as I will be crossing it frequently lengthwise, or else diagonally, without any rule or method" (de Maistre 7). His travel account contains forty-two chapters, some of which sometimes contain only a few lines, one having just two words, as if each chapter comprised a day of his journey and an entry in his logbook. The shortness of the chapters, the absence of dates, and a peculiarly erratic "plot" (if we can even call it that) which only samples a few given hours — all this makes clear that this is a travel diary of a different type of experience, one that cannot simply be put down in chronological and reconstructed manner in order to be followed. Just as his friend Rodolphe Toepffer in his equally successful *Voyages en zigzag* (*Zigzag Journeys*) had to cover even larger distances, and therefore profited greatly from not having an itinerary, so de Maistre traverses his room, back and forth, back and forth, and round and round.

During his wanderings, the "sedentary traveler" (de Maistre 37) not only discovers the functional beauty of everyday things — the many common items of a normal household, such as a bed and an armchair — he also reports on the history of the paintings that hang in the room and on what he finds in his small library. Mostly, de Maistre reports casually on the narrative unfolding of

CHAPITRE XII.

le tertre

01.0 Page from Xavier de Maistre, *Voyage autour de ma chambre*; in de Maistre, *Œuvres complètes*, illustrated by G. Staal, new ed. (Paris, no date), 27.

each day—be it about his servant, his dog, or his lovers—narratives in which, through the mindset of the traveler, a special receptivity or sensibility results where "this very dichotomy, 'boring daily life' pitted against 'marvellous world'" (de Botton 248), is uniquely suspended. The everyday is transformed through the specific perspective of the journey around the room into specific narratives that are indeed about the power of the habitual, which for the brief period of the journey loses its power.

Xavier de Maistre limits his journey exclusively to the space of his room. The view from the window, which soon would become a literary *topos* (see the Fifth Leg), plays as limited a role as do the building's environs, which are completely erased. Instead, the journey is first and foremost about the interior of the room and the interiority of the experience of the one who "travels around" (de Maistre, *Nouvelles*, 28). The result is that these are turned into newly discovered realms removed from the world.

The room itself is a "delightful country that holds every good thing, and all the riches of life" (de Maistre 67), and needs nothing more than itself. A world before the fall of man, innocent as a result of its brief *splendid isolation*, is briefly taken out of time and yet still loaded with history. Here he makes, as he writes, "discovery after discovery" (de Maistre 21). De Maistre is thus the opposite of the immensely popular "Robinsonade" of the late eighteenth and early nineteenth centuries.* While Robinson Crusoe—no matter the version, of which there are many—on his deserted island in the far-off and not-so-placid ocean recapitulates the social and cul-

---

* This comparison can also be found in one of the first monographs on de Maistre from 1918: "One thing is clear, it's not necessary to be completely isolated, such as a Pellico or a Crusoe, in order, with the greatest of ease, to become fond of the small things of our own limited world, and thus with friends to raise a toast to them with a lightly joking and pleasant demeanor. All that is required is to be young, a friend of both conviviality and solitude, and to feel oneself momentarily robbed of freedom" (Berthier 48).

tural patterns of his native land, examining them and then asserting them anew, the room traveler explores with his alienated gaze all the familiar property and objects of an isolated and yet centrally located dwelling in the middle of a city, transforming everything without altering any of it. Everything remains in its place. The traveler doesn't arrange anything that is around him anew, but instead studies its normal function with his gaze. None of the objects are strange, only the gaze that meets them. It is what returns to them the measure of strangeness they have lost to the quotidian. Objects are the familiar-strange compass points of his travel account and his life, which as it flows from the objects, allows itself to be told.

Inside the room, de Maistre also undertakes the kind of introspection that leads to a particular kind of metaphysical model, which then further informs the journey. He discovers that he is "double," that he consists of a thinking soul and a body, which he describes as *the other*. "Never have I been more clearly aware that I am *double*" (de Maistre 67). Not only are both observed by him, but each can observe the other. Thus the "most astonishing metaphysical tour de force that man can perform [is] . . . to give his soul the task of examining the doings of the beast, and to watch it at work without joining in" (de Maistre 12). Here again are the parallels of movement and standing still, of that which is our own and that which is other, of familiarity and distance, that inform his stance throughout. And so the hidden goal of the journey is also "to send his soul off on its travels all by itself" (de Maistre 13). Xavier de Maistre's journey around his room is recognizable as a journey of a soul that opens up an inner world of freedom and self-actualization amid the spatial limitations of his own four walls. "They have forbidden me to roam around a city, a mere point in space; but they have left me with the whole universe: immensity and eternity are mine to command" (de Maistre 66). In his later foreword, de Maistre also ironically comments on this discovery as anticipating transcendental philosophy, which can be found only

I.

A Book of Discoveries.

WHAT more glorious than to open for one's self a new career, — to appear suddenly before the learned world with a book of discoveries in one's hand, like an unlooked-for comet blazing in the empyrean!

No longer will I keep my book in obscurity. Behold it, gentlemen; read it! I have undertaken and performed a forty-two days' journey round my room. The interesting observations I have made, and the constant pleasure I have experienced all along the road, made me wish to publish my travels; the certainty of being

1

01.1 Xavier de Maistre, "A Book of Discoveries"; in de Maistre, *A Journey around My Room* (New York, 1871).

in the gaze of one who journeys about his room. "Metaphysics is a science that seldom mentions the traveler: yet with a famous exception, namely that which occurs in the *Voyage autour de ma maison* [sic!], one finds within it a complete system of transcendental philosophy, such that any of those women who do not like and hardly ever read weighty tomes will end up knowing just as much about the critique of the soul as the famous Professor Kant" (de Maistre, *Nouvelles*, 28).

De Maistre's journey around his room is, if we follow further the allusion to Kant, a critique of reason in regard to the traveler who discovers what it means to travel in place, and with it the gaze of the other upon a supposedly familiar realm of experience. Two hundred years after de Maistre's journey, Daniel Leuwers writes about trips with his grandfather to Beauvais, where Xavier de Maistre wrote his account, and arrives at this wonderful formulation: "The room is an ideal place to withdraw [*retrait*]—more so than a place to simply retreat and retire [*retraite*]" (Leuwers 103).

Travel Reading

Anon. Review of *Voyage autour de ma chambre*. *Journal de Paris*, no. 244. 20 May 1796. 977f.

Becker, Claudia. *Zimmer-Kopf-Welten: Motivgeschichte des Interieurs im 19. und 20. Jahrhundert*. Munich, 1990. 31–41.

Berthier, Alfred. *Xavier de Maistre: Etude biographique et littéraire*. No place, 1918.

Botton, Alain de. *The Art of Travel*. New York, 2004.

Covin, Michel. Préface. *Xavier de Maistre, Expédition nocturne autour de ma chambre*. Mayenne, 1990. 7–19.

Grisar, Albert. *Voyage autour de ma chambre*. Paris, 1859.

Heller, Stephen, composer. *Voyage autour de ma chambre for Piano*, op. 140. 1875.

Jaquet, Friedrich David. *Reise in meinem Zimmer in den Jahren 1812 und 1813*. Riga, 1813.

Labiche and Delacour. *Voyage autour de ma marmite*. First edition. Paris, Théatre du Palais-Royal. 29 November 1859 (= *Théatre contemporain illustré, 523e et 524e livraisons*).

Leuwers, Daniel. "Le Voyage immobile." In Leuwers, *Le Voyage immobile*. Saint-Estève, 2001. 103–14.

Maistre, Xavier de. *A Journey around My Room*. Trans. Alan Brown. London, 2004.

———. *Lettres à sa famille*. Ed. Gabriel de Maistre. 3 vols. Clermond-Ferrand, 2005 (vol. 1) and 2006 (vols. 2 and 3).

———. *Lettre de M. De S — — à M. Le Comte de C — — off— — dans la Légion des Campements*. Chambéry, 1784.

———. Préface des éditeurs. In de Maistre, *Nouvelles*. Ed. Pierre Dumas et al. Geneva, 1984. 27–30.

Maistre, Xavier de, and Joseph de Maistre. *Prospectus de l'expérience aérostatique de Chambéry*. Chambéry, 1784.

Perin, René. *Le Voyage autour de ma chambre: Vaudeville en un acte*. Paris, 1816.

Poujol, Adolphe, and Edouard Scheidig. *Voyage autour de ma chambre: Monologue melée de chants, représentée sur le théatre du gymnase des enfants*. Paris, 1851.

Rey, Luc. *Xavier de Maistre: Sa vie et ses œuvres*. Chambéry, 1865.

Sangsue, Daniel. *Le Récit excentrique*. Paris, 1987.

Sterne, Laurence. *A Sentimental Journey through France and Italy*. London, 1768.

Toepffer, Rodolphe. *Nouveaux voyages en zigzag*. Paris, 1813.

———. *Voyages en zigzag*. Paris, 1843.

Vissière, Isabelle, and Jean-Louis Vissière. "Un micro-genre littéraire: 'Le voyage autour de ma chambre.'" *Lettres et réalités: Mélanges de littérature générale et de critique romanesque offerts au professeur Henri Coulet par ses amis*. Aix-en-Provence, 1988. 417–30.

Pilgrimages

Travel, as I do, around your own little room, asking yourself
what's really there, neglecting nothing at all during your
search, and when you arrive at the end of your journey, look
inside yourself and ask if you don't feel more benevolent,
civilized, charitable, industrious, and in a word, better and
thus happier than you did before.

Faucon, x

And you, my monk's cell, my sweet and dearly loved domicile,
I love you, for I, like Pascal, am convinced that most of our
sorrows come from not spending enough time in our room.

Vuillemin, 189

Traveling through Islamic countries today, we often see drawings
on the whitewashed walls, or even large-scale paintings that depict a journey in several or many individual scenes. Thus we find
on a whitewashed clay wall in the Farafra Oasis, which lies on
the western end of Egypt and several hours outside Cairo in the
middle of the Libyan Desert, pictures of ships and airplanes, of
cars and buses. These show the observer that whoever lives there
has successfully completed the Hajj, the pilgrimage to Mecca that
should be undertaken by all religious Muslims at least once in a
lifetime. They also attest to, in so many words, the soteriological
status of the believer, the chances of his eventual salvation having

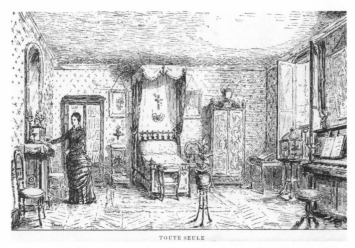

02.0 *Toute Seule* (All alone); in Marie O'Kennedy, *Inventaire de ma chambre*, with engravings by F. Paillet, revised and augmented 3rd ed. (Paris, 1887), 14.

been substantially improved as a result of the journey — and because such a journey is quite expensive, the evidence of his material wealth. Pilgrimages also have a long tradition in Christianity and many other world religions. Yet sometimes there are many serious reasons that prevent such pilgrimages, be they wars, illness, or simply lack of material means. What, then, can one do when so much, if not everything, is at stake in making such a journey? In the Christian tradition, we find a peculiar device that simulates the distant journey, making it possible for the traveler to remain close to home and yet still travel. It's the so-called Sacri Monti, a "topographical simulation of sacred sites" that employs life-size, painted terra-cotta figures (Grau 42). In Varallo alone there are forty-three chapels. Around 1500, this became a model for other pilgrimage sites, and until the mid-nineteenth century one could find numerous such sites in northern Italy. All one had to do was walk a little ways or travel just a few kilometers, and yet still take in all the major holy sites — and thus come much closer to salvation. In 1488, Pope Innocent VIII even granted an indulgence to pil-

02.1 Sacri Monti in Rapallo.

grims to Varallo. Many later popes followed this example well into the eighteenth century — occasionally coupling it with a so-called plenary indulgence granted by Clemens VIII in 1599. Even today, above the portal of the church in Domodossola is an inscription indicating the indulgence granted in a specific year (Landgraf 25f.).

Yet souls also wander far and with pleasure. The journey of the soul is a *topos* of nearly every world religion. And even during life, the demands of the soul's postmortem journey cast their dark shadows upon earthly existence. If life as such is already a journey, then that journey becomes all the more complex, having from the very beginning to consider the final actual goal. This brings us to Antoine Caillot's lovely formulation on the occasion of a journey that he made in 1809 among the four major Parisian cemeteries, a circuit encompassing "everywhere and nowhere at once" (Caillot 41). All such earthly journeys are a faint reflection of the real journey that still remains ahead. The notion of being only a guest on earth and only after death finding one's true home in heaven

02.2 Sacri Monti in Rapallo.

was, in the Christian tradition, the chronological-eschatological framework that underscored the irreducible tentativeness of the earthly journey. "Humans are only travelers upon the earth, even though many wish to settle upon it; but a Christian must see the earth as a place of exile and misery: he should endlessly address his sighs towards Heaven in order to remember his true home" (Anon., *Voyage spirituel*, no page).

Yet when all of earthly life is only a form of exile, the room journey — in whatever way it occurs — at least offers a form of security: the traditional idea that the body is a house in which the soul supposedly resides, something which in Paulist theology, as formulated in the First Letter to the Corinthians, also finds its continuation in Christianity, thus also serving as a spatial metaphor that turns each room into an analogy for human existence and grants a sense of home. Viewed as such, a room traveler can, *through the means by which he travels his room*, also accompany his own body with his soul in order to prepare both body and soul for the great journey, and at the same time bring order to the transitory nature of life. The Christian room traveler beholds inside his room the material and spatial manifestation of his life's journey and consequently the analogy of the earthly-bodily shell that contains his soul.

When earthly journeys are then conceived as precursors to the final journey, and their trials and tribulations seen as a kind of orientation for it, the journey around one's room seriously transforms the contingency and meaninglessness of life into order and meaning, as well as time into space. In the Christian sense, next to the pilgrim there is only one other true traveler: the room traveler. In his early life, he prepares himself in an immediate sense for the final journey by traveling, reflecting, testing, meditating, praying, and not least of all, questioning. The wandering involved with the earthly journey doesn't apply to him. His journey is from the start a form of stationary observation, which ideally prepares him for what will occur after his death. Traveling in place.

Thus we readily find in the monastic tradition the comparison of meditation in a monk's cell to a journey. "The *xeniteia* the monks experience in their cells is equal to *peregrinato in stabilitate*" (Barthes 208). And therefore it is no surprise that in nineteenth-century literature we find some explicitly *Catholic* room journeys, as well as a good number of other such journeys that have a theological grounding. Léon Gautier's *Voyage d'un catholique autour de sa chambre* (*A Catholic's Journey around His Room*) from the mid-nineteenth century thus also recalls first and foremost the prayers that Christian churches have devoted to human dwellings,* in which we can see the true depiction of a room journey in the transformation of a room into a church, and thus into a temple that in two ways, both above and below, reveals the microcosm and the macrocosm, the single individual as well as the great order, and

---

* "Among these blessings there are several that address human dwellings. . . . We have reflected a good while upon these wonderful formulations, and we cite them in order to share with our readers what meaning the church ascribes to the room, and what idea we can arrive at as a result" (Gautier 16).

opens up interchangeable realms: room, body, and cathedral are realms between which the room traveler can journey. The room can become the body and the cathedral. The body can become the room and the cathedral. The cathedral can become the room and the body. When the traveler crosses the room, he can also travel through his body and a cathedral. The Christian blessing *Christus mansionem benedicat*, Christ bless this house, encompasses like a Russian nesting doll a space within a space within a space and compresses body, room, and cathedral all into one.

Through this particular transformation of space, the room attains a meaning unavailable to the secular gaze or the heathen: "There where the economist and the native see nothing more than 'shelter,' a sanctuary exists. It invites us to observe our room as a *place* that unites within itself various sacraments" (Gautier 11). And thus it's hardly any wonder that amid such a journey the room resembles a window of a gothic cathedral (Gautier 19), the body-room-cathedral being a sacred place, a place of sacraments, a place of sacrifice and healing, a place of promise and deliverance. Room, body, and cathedral demonstrate the long-familiar philosophical principle: "Beauty is the radiance of truth" (Gautier 63).

In light of this transformation, each object also gains a special meaning and can be transformed in its own right. The Christian room journey is a spiritual transubstantiation of its contents, which take on enormous meaning as a result of it. Each single object within the room that is a leg of life's journey that should become the soul's journey is an object for unremitting meditation on life as a journey. Thus, like the believer who sometimes can pass through the stations of the cross in a church, the Christian room journey recapitulates the stations of one's life with the help of the objects within one's room, resulting in an *Imitatio Christi* that travels through a room. And this occurs in a well-ordered world. We need only read some of the very Catholic *Nouveau voyage autour de ma chambre*, which, in never failing to mention the extremely theocratic governance of this little realm, divides the world of one's room into provinces: "Like Eugénie de Guérin, I love my room because I can make of it what I wish: a parlor, a church, an academy. In fact, within this kingdom there are three provinces: that of prayer, of work, and of rest. The most important towns of the province of prayer are Christ and his mother, the *prie-dieu*, memories, etc. In the province of work the best-known towns are the tool cabinet, the library, the pen, the inkwell, the piano, etc. The last province, that of rest, is more cheery than the others, for there one witnesses the most prized locations, such as the fireplace, the grandfather clock, the mirror, and above all my lovely white bed. My nations also have colonies: the wardrobe, the balcony, etc. Lovely small rooms entirely suffused with the scents of the blessings of the church, recalling the most splendid of palaces. You are my Louvre, my Tuileries, my Vatican, and much more. To me you are much more than a palace, you are a kingdom of which I am queen, etc. You are, like a saint so fittingly put it, the gate to heaven. Therefore you will not be surprised if I wander through your provinces, study your beauty, breathe in your scents, and listen to your valued teachings" (Vuillemin 23).

We see already in this brief description the particular meaning that is granted to things. They are what structure the passage through the room's narrative and thus, to stick with the metaphor, are what make up the beads of the praying traveler's rosary. This is also what leads to the peculiar poetry of lists that we find among such Christian journeys, the most impressive perhaps being Marie O'Kennedy's *Inventaire de ma chambre* (*An Inventory of My Room*) from 1884, a text that right from the start alludes to other room journeys in order to link itself in one way or another to them. Léon Gautier's *Voyage d'un catholique autour de sa chambre* is the most important of these references. The programmatic inventory of the room begins in O'Kennedy's book, whose protagonist is a seventeen-year-old girl, with a detailed description of the crucifix,

CHAPITRE VII.

Une croix de bois.

'OU vient cette croix de bois? Vous devinez peut-être. C'est un morceau de la porte d'une maison religieuse fracturée par le crocheteur. Vous désirez sans doute apprendre comment la chose s'est passée. Eh bien! écoutez. C'était. . . .

. . . . ,

Et ils s'en allaient disant: S'ils nous chassent de nos demeures, ils ne nous chasseront pas du ciel.

02.3 "Une croix de bois" (A wooden cross); in R. P. Dom. J. B. Vuillemin, *Nouveau voyage autour de ma chambre* (no place, 1894): 82.

though it doesn't neglect to describe the font for holy water, and finally concludes a good three hundred pages later with a description of the *prie-dieu*. Any instructive travel reading cannot neglect such diligence. The Christian journal *Bulletin de la Sociéte generale d'Education* offers "scholarly and literary travel" (O'Kennedy 9) parallel to that which O'Kennedy carries out within her room. The pilgrimage through one's room, during which, in reaching back to a distant Christian metaphor, the narrator transforms in the course of the contemplative journey a cell or birdcage into a beehive, has stages in the presentation of things, such that the room journey allows the self to pass by objects in an orderly sequence whose decided goal is to reveal an unknown world behind the visible world of appearances, and thus to discover a soul within oneself.

The text is therefore full of lists that arrange things in relation to one another: objects that are not what they appear to be, but rather are meant more to gradually prepare the traveler for the observation, as well as the use, of the *prie-dieu* with which the journey concludes. Such lists — like this one among many — read as follows:

My bed
My armoire
My piano, and so on and so forth! . . .
My sewing basket
My mirror
My table
My painting, etc. etc. (O'Kennedy 32)

O'Kennedy, however, also lists each single gem on the crucifix — in order, as she quotes from Paul, to savor these things, as if they have never been savored (O'Kennedy 42), in order to discover the wonder that the contemplation offered by such a journey reveals, while at the same time appreciating it as a symbol of earthly transience before the cross.

In Emma Faucon's *Voyage d'une jeune fille autour de sa chambre* (*A Young Girl's Journey around Her Room*), which appeared some twenty years earlier, it's not a young girl who undertakes a room journey but rather an old woman who, in the middle of her room and all its objects, recalls her childhood and asks herself, "Why all these memories that are so clear and definite, why have such remote events from the past to some extent taken on new life and nearly found again the intensity of reality?" (Faucon vii f.). Through her reflections, this Christian traveler also transforms things into objects of contemplation and into allegories of her life. Thus space becomes time and objects become history. Memory is so permeated with facts that there appears a hitherto imperceptible moral, a previously unrecognized necessity: "Experience is memory thought through. . . . Nothing is according to chance, everything is logically ordered amid the beautiful order of creation" (Faucon vii f.). A word is sometimes all that is needed to make such order apparent. A thing can provide a revelation. And this then reveals the order of the entire world. Everything then has meaning: "In order to grasp it, all that is needed is to turn one's attention to any object" (Faucon ix f.). Any room, and thus nature as well, is transformed into an open book in which good and evil are set down and are legible to anyone. And the same is true for the complete range of objects of contemplation in the preordained world: the window and the garden beyond the image of the *Crucified Christ* by Lucas Signorelli from 1512, which as a gift from his father provides both a paternal memory and exhortation, or the mirror that reveals "true beauty," or the library with its ordered shelves. The "junk room [*capharnaüm*] of my apartment" (Faucon 83) with its things bought or received as gifts, such as the porcelain dog from the parish fair, as a "manifestation of the endless powers of nature" becomes an "embryo of the world" (Faucon 101); while the piano or the desk or the commode cannot remain just a thing in itself, but must become what it stands for. Things then become, like the room, the body, and the cathedral, allegories of the order of the world, a continuous "treasure chest" whose value is primarily attested to through Christian revelation. And this treasure, over the course of continuous modernization, stands on the brink of disappearing forever: "Earlier one had a sense of home, but today that is nearly gone. Yet where is the world headed amid this dizzying rush of things? What's the point of it all? What drives it on? Alas!" Thus laments the room traveler while also providing the reader with a moral and spiritual remedy and recommending the path to moral goodness: "There are always two paths that are simultaneously present. The one leads quickly to the good, but it is rare; the other offers the pleasures that the masses seek, be they fame, fortune, money, everything but the most important things. As a believer in travel and in staying at home, I satisfy this two-fold disposition, which seems contradictory, by taking a journey through my room. In this humble land there is also something to see, to observe, and above all to absorb. Every person, according to Abbé Perreyve, who has circled the world twice has probably discovered less than the poor hermit who has taken a journey through his room" (Vuillemin 5f.).

Travel Reading

Anon. *Voyage spirituel.* No place, 1817 (Bibliothèque Nationale/ Paris: BN D-54711).

Barthes, Roland. *Wie zusammen leben.* Frankfurt am Main, 2007.

Caillot, Antoine. *Voyage religieux et sentimental aux quatre cimiti-ères de Paris.* Paris, 1809.

Faucon, Emma. *Voyage d'une jeune fille autour de sa chambre.* Paris, 1864.

Gautier, Léon. *Voyage d'un catholique autour de sa chambre.* Paris, 1862.

Grau, Oliver. *Virtual Art.* Trans. Gloria Custace. Cambridge, 2003.

Landgraf, Gabriele. *Die Sacri Monti in Piedmont und in der Lombar-dei: Zwischen Wirklichkeitsillusion und Einbeziehung der Primär-realität.* Frankfurt am Main, 2000 (= Europäische Hochschul-schriften, series 28, Kunstgeschichte, vol. 362).

Navery, Raoul de. *Voyage dans une église*. Paris, 1863.

O'Kennedy, Marie. *Inventaire de ma chambre*. Third edition. Paris, 1887 (first edition, Paris, 1884).

Vuillemin, J. B., R. P. Dom. *Nouveau voyage autour de ma chambre*. Second edition. No place, 1894.

The "Frauenzimmer"

THE FRAUENZIMMER EYE — n. There are certain things where the Frauenzimmer's eye for things is sharper than those of a hundred men. Lessing 1, 408.

Entry in *Grimms' Dictionary*

Books and travel were for me the only complete blessings of this life.

La Roche, 1788, 190

Has it never before occurred to you how easily the idea of travel can distract me from my daily duties?

La Roche, 1799, 1:204

"Frauenzimmer — n. from the early Gothic *timr*, *timbr*, Old High German *zimpar* meaning *wood*, *timber*, the constructed building, the apartment, the chamber. A Frauenzimmer is thus a woman's chamber, a woman's room, a woman's parlor, where women or wives gather, where they can converse, also where they work." Thus notes *Grimms' Dictionary* under the heading of "Frauenzimmer," after which it comments on the specific definition that the term implies: "Frauenzimmer refers to the collective group of people who live within it, such as the female servants, the attendants to the princess, just as the court encompasses the members of court, and the village the farmers who live in it. . . . More precisely, this general definition also applied not to women who lived together in a specific chamber, but rather to women who were generally thought of as well mannered. . . . Interestingly enough, the reference to the individual eventually evolved out of the collective reference, much in the manner taken on by words like 'lad' or 'comrade.' The 'Frauenzimmer' refers first to a place, then to a number of women of court, then to individuals, and finally to a dignified, educated woman."

The journey of this word runs from a spatial descriptor to the collective to the individual, and at the end of the eighteenth century this occurs again in reference to room travel, in which the three different entities are bound together. Whenever a "Frauenzimmer" undertakes a journey through her room, it also involves exploring the conditions of an individual female through the collective terms used to describe it. The journey runs, so to say, through the verbal history of the space (the room), to the collective (the "Frauenzimmer" as a general descriptor), to the individual (in the sense of a collective and the history that makes it such), yet it repeats these stages through the figure of a journey's topography, which unifies all three dimensions of the word *Frauenzimmer* in the gaze leveled at the objects of the room.

We find such a journey in the writings of Sophie La Roche. In the journal published by her, *Pomona für Teutschlands Töchter* (*Pomona — For Germany's Daughters*), she answers the "questions about my room" with a detailed, multipage description of "my room and my view" (La Roche 1783–84, 227). In *Mein Schreibtisch* (*My Desk*), which appeared fifteen years later, this description has already taken on other dimensions.

"Whether or not the 'Frauenzimmer' should be allowed to travel" is a question posed by Franz Ludwig Posselt in 1795 in his book *Apodemik oder die Kunst zu reisen* (*Apodemic; or, The Art of Travel*). And this question is posed anew — though now with a dif-

Mein Schreibetisch.

von

Sophie von La Roche.

An Herrn H. R. F. in D.

erstes Bändchen.

Leipzig 1799.

bey Heinr. Gräff.

03.0 Frontispiece to Sophie La Roche, *Mein Schreibtisch*, vol. 2 (Karben, 1997, reprint of the 1799 Leipzig edition).

ferent aim — by Annegret Pelz in her lovely book *Reisen durch die eigene Fremde* (*Journey through My Own Strange Land*), in which Sophie La Roche appears as one of the first to travel through her own interior. In it, La Roche's two-volume book *Mein Schreibtisch*, which "until now had not been included among the author's travel accounts" (Pelz 49), is included among those room journeys from the end of the eighteenth century that Gender Studies has designated as a specific form of female writing (see Gudrun Loster-Schneider's extended discussion), and that are not about the infinity and irreducible sovereignty of the inner life but rather concern themselves much more with socially determined and culturally coded constraints. In *Mein Schreibtisch*, La Roche appears, according to Pelz, as somewhat of a "collector of her own self. That which is distant in time and space is collected as correspondence, books, and objects of memory 'all together in the capsule' of her interior" (Pelz 50). Here also there appears the experimental formation of the miniature journey as a way of crossing distance through observation, more precisely as a "process of radical self-alienation" in which the room is transformed into the "exterior of one's own head." "Thought of in this way, the head can be seen more objectively, and one can travel through it" (Pelz 53). The "Frauen-Zimmer," according to Pelz, becomes the "Head-Room," the exploration of which leads to one's own sense of self-estrangement.

Sophie La Roche had indeed undertaken numerous journeys, and written and published extensive accounts of them, including trips through Switzerland, Holland, and England, as well as a trip "from Offenbach to Weimar and Schöneck in 1799." She missed only Italy, she noted, "the fatherland of the wonders of the nature of art" (La Roche 1799, 1:363). The reason why was the death of her son, though at the end of the first volume of *Mein Schreibtisch*, she devotes twenty pages to imagining what it must be like, her soul nonetheless "so fulfilled, that I really dreamed of such pleasures, and then wrote about them when I awoke" (La Roche 1799, 1:363f.), perhaps in the hope "that wishes and plans are already pleasures in themselves, since usually through such writing, which is bound up with desire through impatience, the reader arrives at a quiet sense of expectation" (La Roche 1799, 1:168f.).

The Italian journey she imagined and wrote down is only one of the legs of the journey around her room that La Roche undertook in her two-volume and over 850-page encyclopedic book *Mein Schreibtisch*, one that at no point leaves the four walls of her room, and is completely restricted to her writing desk and library. It offers itself up as the fulfillment of a request by a "noble friend" who so loved to enter "my little room with its desk and beloved books and pictures" (La Roche 1799, 1:1f.) that he asked if it were possible for her to give him a precise description of this room. "The room in which you spend such a large part of your days" was so valued by him that he, La Roche goes on to say, fostered the wish to "know all of these different objects" (La Roche 1799, 1:2). And he asked her as well for "an entirely faithful description of this desk and the window adjacent to it without, however much she may wish to, altering, removing, or adding anything, no matter how disadvantageous or advantageous I might think it to do so" (La Roche 1799, 1:3). Yet is the fulfillment of such a promise at all possible? The "Frauenzimmer" is indeed so complex, multilayered, and rich with various things that it makes it difficult to arrive at a detailed description. Nevertheless, La Roche takes him at his word and begins with an unusual litany, which Gudrun Loster-Schneider faithfully summarizes (in the process of which it is quoted extensively): "La Roche begins with the description of the way she has organized her desk and the things that sit on top of it. Some almanacs that are not mentioned again, a file for personal papers, previously read issues of the 'Ladies Magazine,' seven fascicles with excerpts from predominantly foreign authors. Next to these are more books that the narrator characterizes explicitly as 'abiding neighbors': Burke's *Essay on the Sublime and Beautiful*, Thomson's *The Sea-*

sons, Miremont's *Education des femmes*, Young's *Night Thoughts*,
Lessing's 'The Education of the Human Race,' Ankenside's 'lovely
work on the imagination,' Plato's *Letters*, and Kant's *Observations
on the Feeling of the Beautiful and the Sublime*. Among further diverse and small items, whose status as printed works or excerpts
remains unclear, she cites d'Alembert, Rochefoucault, Mirabeau,
Maintenon, and Sévigné. Finally there follows a collection of titles
of wished-for books. The conclusion consists of the already noted
'mish-mash' of recipes, aphorisms, poems, and portraits. In the
next sequence the view is turned to the desktop where two stacks
of fascicles lie. One of the stacks consists mostly of copies of German, French, and English poems, moral aphorisms, and special-
ized texts from various academic disciplines. The other stack presents on the other hand a portfolio of used editions of Goldsmith's
The Deserted Village, a fascicle with letters from Julie Bondelis, and
exposed at the end, her ongoing correspondence. Towards the end
of the text the view slips, as expected, away from the desk to an
inventory of the library" (Loster-Schneider 299).

Indeed, this summary makes clear the dimensions of Sophie
La Roche's undertaking. What began as a supposedly humble
wish has now become a nearly titanic undertaking. As a result, La
Roche doesn't lose sight of the definition of *Frauenzimmer* listed in
Grimms' Dictionary that recalls the "ancient Gothic *timr*, *timbr*, and
the Old High German *zimpar* meaning *wood*." Her desk is made of
"wood from the old regional forest" of the House of Warthausen
(La Roche 1799, 1:9), and, as she adds ruefully, "it has been with
me through all my days!" (La Roche 1799, 1:17). The description of
the layers heaped on the desk turns into a virtual paleontology of
her own history, while as part of the stratographic survey of her
individual "Frauenzimmer," the exercise of composing "a straight-
forward description of the mixture of papers and books spread out
on this desk next to the window" also assumes that she will indeed
have to provide to her "noble friend" a "very precise blueprint

03.1 Georg Friedrich Kersting, *Woman Writing a Letter inside a Room*, 1817; in Sabine Schulze, ed., *Innenleben: Die Kunst des Intérieurs; Vermeer bis Kabakov* (Ostfildern-Ruit, 1998), 179.

of my own thought and inclinations" (La Roche 1799, 1:6). *Mein Schreibtisch* encompasses not only "a type of inner biography" (Milch 187) but rather, as Annegret Pelz puts it well, an external "auto-geography" of that very existence that is relinquished amid any introspection, and that ultimately is limited to the various writings found on and around her desk in her "Frauenzimmer."

Postscript

The artist Monika Pichler has in several of her exhibitions used the peculiar term *Frauenzimmer* as a means to explore its relationship to travel, specifically room travel. In doing so, she works with carpets, although she does not weave them or tie them; instead they are composed as silk screens that only superficially look like carpets. The carpet with its associations of nomadic as well as domestic existence serves thus as a reflection on the historical constraints on the "Frauenzimmer" in terms of travel. Or in the words of Pichler: "The inspiration for the exhibition 'Frauen-zimmer — Zimmerreise' is the fact that in the nineteenth century the opportunity for travel was very limited. The travel accounts of those who nonetheless managed to step beyond the borders of the household were greeted with sharp interest; their books sold numerous copies in providing the opportunity for others to experience what they had at home. Reading these accounts today, it is nearly impossible to compare them to the places they describe, because over time most of the places and landscapes have changed so much — thus making it only possible to visit them by traveling at home. The view of 'the past' also sharpens the appreciation of 'the present,' just as the view of 'the other' also contains the view of 'onself.' Travels in the Orient provided women of the eighteenth and nineteenth centuries the opportunity to enter and write about spaces (such as harems) that men kept closed off. I have selected five types of travel interiors for this exhibition and made portraits, carpets, and pillows for each in order to create an oriental ambience. Also included in the installation is a small number of books I have collected in recent years. Visitors thus have the opportunity to pick up a book and to sit, lie, lounge on the bench, and read, as well as forget that one is in a museum, and travel to the Orient instead" (Pichler 2004).

Travel Reading

Das Deutsche Wörterbuch von Jakob und Wilhelm Grimm. http://germazope.uni-trier.de/Projects/DWB.

La Roche, Sophie von. *Mein Schreibtisch*. 2 vols. Karben, 1997 (reprint of first edition, Leipzig, 1799).

———. *Pomona für Teutschlands Töchter*. 4 vols. Munich, 1987 (reprint of first edition, Speyer, 1783–84).

———. *Tagebuch einer Reise durch Holland und England*. Offenbach, 1788.

Loster-Schneider, Gudrun. *Sophie La Roche: Paradoxien weiblichen Schreibens im 18. Jahrhundert*. Tübingen, 1995. 293–344.

Milch, Werner. *Sophie La Roche—Die Großmutter der Brentanos*. Frankfurt am Main, 1935.

Pelz, Annegret. *Reisen durch die eigene Fremde: Reiseliteratur von Frauen als autogeographische Schriften*. Köln, Weimar, Vienna, 1993. 46–67.

Pichler, Monika. *Installation "Frauenzimmer—Zimmerreise" (Kunstpavillon Innsbruck, 3 January 2004 until 10 April 2004)*. http://www.kuenstlerschaft.at/kue/modules.php?op=modload&name=PagEd&file=index&page_id=359.

Posselt, Franz Ludwig. *Apodemik oder die Kunst zu reisen*. 2 vols. Leipzig, 1795.

Rathenböck, Vera. *Reisen im Wohnzimmer: Die "Teppiche" der Textilkünstlerin Monika Pichler*. http://www.monikapichler.at/.

FOURTH LEG

Expeditions in the Near-at-Hand

I've never really understood the traveler's concerns. I've never found anything in another country that you couldn't find in the same form right in your own street. Many people have gone to America to look at trees, or traveled to China to discover new people. The only excuse the traveler has for going so far away in order to see what's right outside his window is that one cannot lie about what is visible to everyone else. The only serious journey that has any meaning and which can be ever be written about is unquestionably the *Voyage autour de ma chambre*.

Karr, 345

The urge to travel is a sickness from which one can never recover; I myself am evidence of that.

Anon., *Voyage dans mes poches*, 9

There can be many reasons for a room journey: sickness or accident; lack of money or agoraphobia; boredom or melancholy; educational desire or a love of books; thirst, as with any journey, which leads you into your own wine cellar to empty bottle after bottle;* or simply the desire to do just what Xavier de Maistre did.

---

* J. Brot, *Voyage autour de ma cave* (*A Journey around My Cellar*), no place, year, or page: "Scattered across the globe are the fruitful tiers and gleaming hillsides that I always love to look at anew the moment the dawn meanders across our plateaus

04.0 "General view of my realm"; in Arthur Mangin, *Voyage scientifique autour de ma chambre*, revised and augmented 3rd ed. (Paris, 1889), 9.

Among all these various travels, one thing is the same: they describe the exploration of the near-at-hand as a virtual journey of discovery, as an expedition into a supposedly familiar world which suddenly through the lens of travel is transformed, made strange and resistant, puzzling and instructive. Yet in all the room travels of the nineteenth century, the near world remains a comfort despite its strangeness, becoming never a threat or menace but rather much larger, broader, more capacious, and, not the least, richer. Such an expedition is not one into strange lands but rather one into the strangeness of the familiar. Habit makes us blind, travel opens our eyes. And with these new eyes the familiar world is transformed into a cosmos, one both familiar and strange, simultaneously constricted and endless.

---

and bathes them in white light. O geography, I wager that you cannot impose upon me your maps and plans; I have no need of world maps, tables, compass, portolan chart. With no worry about being shipwrecked, without having to navigate by the stars, I commence a long journey in the depths of my wine cellar."

"Mein Zimmer, eine kleine Welt" ("My Room, a Little World") is the title of a chapter in an unauthorized edition of de Maistre's journey published in Basel, which appeared in 1798 under the title *Neue Reise in meinem Zimmer* (*New Journey around My Room*), and which immediately propagated a wonderful formula for the attitude with which one should travel through a room or a house. The room becomes an actual microcosm, the exploration of it at the drop of a hat filling a book, though even after a hundred pages or so it by no means comes to an end. "I have barely taken four steps," so confesses a room traveler to his surprise, "and the description takes up almost a hundred pages!" (Jaquet 72).

Moreover, the fact that some (and soon countless more) room journeys were already published did not stop such room-travel writers from tackling further journeys — even when the same room is described a bit differently in different books. Thus we find some of the pseudogeographic depiction of the room in de Maistre's journey in altered form in many other descriptions of room journeys, the most prominent of which is probably Friedrich David Jaquet's *Reise in meinem Zimmer in den Jahren 1812 und 1813*. Here the journey rushes about the globe and crosses longitude and latitude at will: "My room lies at the 50th parallel, the 18th second and third interval of latitude, and at the 44th parallel, the 29th tercet and fourth interval of longitude as calculated by Ferro. If one wished to also know its shape, as well as floor area and cubic area, it can be described as oblong in shape, its longer side measuring 18 feet, 9 inches, or 3 linear decimals in length; its area being 439 square feet, 5 square inches and 5 square decimals, while its cubic footage is 4391 cubic feet, 3 cubic inches and five cubic decimals. The main contents are the furnace, the bed, the stools, table, the forte-piano, the desk, library, and other various items" (Jaquet 30).

From the end of the eighteenth century until the late nineteenth century, there survive numerous mini room journeys in which the threshold of a room or house or the borders of a city are not crossed. One travels through a pocket, a tent, or a drawer, or a room by day as well as by night, or one's own library or a large city such as Paris, which, according to the passionate long-distance traveler Arsène Houssaye, remains an unknown world to the Parisians themselves — as does the Palais Royal, which merits an entire journey in itself (Houssaye 230).

This last type of journey was especially good for small children who crossed the city alone or with siblings, whether escorted or without any orientation to the city, thereby gaining a proper initiation to it. Typical of this type of journey is Abbé Saglier's *Voyage d'un enfant à Paris* (*A Child's Journey around Paris*) from 1870. The story in this book takes place in 1853. The publisher and — as we later learn — the protagonist of the book tells not only his own story but also how he came to be a writer by writing the book that we are reading, namely the completed journal of his travels. The nine-year-old Julien travels to Paris with his father, who has business there. Both of them stay with Julien's uncle, Monsieur Le Prevost, who travels around the city with them each day with his chauffeur in order to show Julien all there is to absorb, and to interest him in certain things about which he is "capable of discovering the feeling and thought necessary to fully appreciate them" (Saglier 11). The seven days of this journey turn into a regular initiation rite, at the end of which Julien decides to follow in the footsteps of his father's profession and carry on the family genealogy. The story has a cyclical structure, beginning with the visit to a court in session and ending with a postscript that Julien writes as a student and aspiring lawyer. The journey through Paris passes through not only different "Écoles" but also the school of life. From the École de Droit (whose "Code" serves as a proper primer that helps Julien learn how to write and makes possible the deciphering of social phenomena) they then pass on to the École de Médecine and the École Militaire, and on to the École des Beaux-Arts, the church, and the orphanage. A visit to the observatory has to be canceled because the uncle has a migraine. But this allows time to read another book by Xavier de Maistre, namely *Le Lépreux de la cité d'Aoste* (*The Leper of the City of Aosta*) (Saglier 228 ff.). Indeed, one doesn't have to travel through all of Paris to still have expert guidance, for even a day's journey through a building is enough to achieve a similar kind of initiation. Arthur Mangin's *Voyage scientifique autour de ma chambre* (*A Scientific Journey around My Room*), which is richly illustrated with engravings and had numerous printings in the nineteenth century,[†] set itself the goal of coupling an interest in natural history with that of literature, though without wanting to entirely forsake the latter. The narrator leads the son of a childhood friend, who until then had been devoted to "letters," on a journey through his house and explains to him room by room, object by object, the accomplishments of modern science, which is no longer an arcane, secret knowledge but now available to all. The room is the place in which, according to history, most discoveries are made, and which through the perspective of the journey can be made in other ways: "A room . . . is unquestionably the biggest country on earth, the most multifaceted in its manifestations, the most remarkable and informative site a traveler who is reasonably intelligent can contemplate. All types of discoveries, observations, and studies are possible within it" (Mangin 4). And when he then travels through his house as a guide to his student, he is a philosopher, a historian, a natural scientist, a physicist, and a chemist all in one. All these disciplines form together an encyclopedia of knowledge whose many

---

[†] By which the author made every effort with each new edition to revise his text in order to keep up with the rapid changes and developments, etc., in science. Yet despite the enormous acceleration in knowledge, there is also a continuity, a permanent value to what is depicted that must be stated: "This is the lot of science books today: they age, from one day to the next they become old. That is not encouraging, nor is it my desire to pass on a *journey* to young people that will not last. . . . Yet because I have made sure that my book still contains a certain breath of youth, then perhaps it is possible, with a few adjustments, to present the world as it is without seeming too antiquated" (Mangin viii).

branches he tries to touch upon through his peripatetic passing through and the ensuing dialogue. "Thus one can, just by remaining at home and restraining yourself to a few square meters, travel the entire world, whether it be in the present or in the past" (Mangin 6). The room is an interior world that is in many ways charged with history and an encyclopedic knowledge of the world. A room can be described as a country: with a climate, a location, a form of governance, a people, flora, and fauna. It unfortunately doesn't have flora in the concrete sense, but at least has a view of plants and trees, while instead of fauna there are cats and spiders. In regard to a form of government, a monarchy or, as the case may be, an absolute democracy, "indeed allows its inhabitant to enjoy unlimited power over everything found within his country" (Mangin 10). The legislative and executive branches are controlled by one hand; commerce and industry blossom, the only exports listed being paper that has been written on. Other sights worth seeing are: a library with 450 volumes, an art collection and a natural history museum with six bivalves, an equal number of examples from mineralogy, three stuffed birds, and a snake that is preserved in alcohol. "Here we find the opportunity for a scientific lesson in each single object" (Mangin 25). The journey then moves along *intra muros* according to the "inspiration of the moment and in no methodical order" (Mangin 28), and according to the principle that science exists everywhere. The yellow viper from Martinique provides an imaginary escape to the tropics; other things reflect on the question of what, when, and why something is cold, what "waves" are, and how one must imagine a journey through the universe. The journey through the cabinet of curiosities that is a house ends as well with the universe and the imagined journey into it. In a strange way, the microcosm of the house ends up leading into the endless distance of the macrocosm. The room is transformed into a regular chamber of wonders.

While Mangin undertakes a natural science expedition through

04.1　Spiders; in Arthur Mangin, *Voyage scientifique autour de ma chambre*, revised and augmented 3rd ed. (Paris, 1889), 10.

the world of his house with all of his collections, other journeys take up other strategies by highlighting objects with more or less detailed histories of either an individual or a culture. The *Voyage dans mes poches* (*Journey through My Pockets*) brings to light a tobacco pipe, a handkerchief, balls of wax, and a portfolio that give the opportunity to tell stories attached to them. Alois Schreiber's *Reise meines Vetters auf seinem Zimmer* (*My Cousin's Journey in His Room*), like the pocket journey from 1798, talks about the history of single objects (desk and pen, tobacco pipe and walking stick, hobbyhorse and table, fireplace and poodle) belonging to members of his family or neighbors. In Karl Stern's *Auch eine Reise auf meinem Zimmer* (*Also a Journey around My Room*), which appeared seven years later, the neighbors and their stories are problems that hinder and then impede the journey. "From every corner of my room there steps a memory that is suddenly happy, suddenly sad, and that grips my heart with its chilly hand" (Stern 92f.). And if it's not a painful memory that disrupts the journey, then it's an erotic temptation and its corrective that confront him from across the street, the room traveler in this case inhabiting a house on a corner that grants him a view from two windows: "One of my windows I call Nature and the other I call Art" (Stern 43). The window for Art provides him with an unobstructed view of a young widow; the Nature window looks out onto a mother and child. And because this double view involves such an encryption, it's no wonder that the distance has hardly anything more to offer. For what else can there be to discover?

In contrast, S. D'Houay's 1880 journey through his house announced an expedition similar to Arthur Mangin's that was worthy of the discovery of America. "Is not a house also finally a small universe and can we not expect new interesting discoveries just as in a new America?" (D'Houay 9). And thus the library and the paintings in his apartment are also complete worlds that open up to him. Each object has not only a personal but also a general cultural history. On the journey through his house, the narrator gives himself over to the history of his own culture. The legs of this journey could hardly be more normal than they are heterogeneous: they are about clocks, sugar production, the history of graphic arts; about pianos, coffee, and tobacco; about porcelain, shoes, enamels, and lamps. The cultural and historical information about each of these things does not just reach far into the past, but far away as well. When we begin to reconstruct the history of objects, the near-at-hand is continually transcended. Each single item is in-

04.2 Journey into the forest; in Arthur Mangin, *Voyage scientifique autour de ma chambre*, revised and augmented 3rd ed. (Paris, 1889), 141.

clined as well to allow far-off realms and times into the nearness of the room. The journey of discovery within the room becomes a discovery of distant times and realms. Nor does such discovery follow a fixed plan, but instead jumps like a pinball from thing to thing, from story to story, from anecdote to anecdote. And thus it is also not Xavier de Maistre but rather his friend Rodolphe Toepffer who is the reference point of the journey: "My excursion through the house is truly a zigzag journey" (D'Houay 51).

Toepffer, de Maistre, and not least of all James Cook are the recurring reference points for all these journeys. The comparison of the room journey to Cook's exploratory journey belongs to the *topos* of these stories. Sometimes Cook is a contrasting model used to show that the room is a world still waiting to be discovered; other times, however, merely a form of nighttime reading: "In order that I'm satisfied that nothing is missing, for my own pleasure I have on the wall next to my bed a beautiful map of the world on which the travels of the famous Cook are displayed and detailed, and can, if I turn my head a little, allow me to fantasize that I can walk from the shores of Lake Geneva to the Bosporus, Mount Salève to the Tafelberg—and all that without a shipwreck or any other dangers" (Jourdan 59). And occasionally amid all this, Cook appears as the weary traveler from the time of the zeal for travel, the time for such explorations having indeed passed, there being no more continents to discover, the discoveries made in libraries sufficiently, albeit longwindedly, describing everything, and which one can consult easily. Therefore, the room journey seems entirely appropriate: within our "somewhat aimless and soundlessly mellifluous lives" (Stern 117), we "seek in the distance what usually lies right in front of us, indeed already in our own hearts!" (Stern 110). We no longer need to go on a lengthy exploration, but rather remain at home and examine our surroundings closely in order to travel well.

Among the *ad nauseam* profusion of countless travel accounts at the end of the eighteenth century, there are ironic texts that react against this Cook mania, such as Louis Balthazard Néel's *Voyage de Paris à Saint-Cloud par mer, et retour de Saint-Cloud à Paris, par terre* (*The Journey from Paris to Saint Cloud by Sea and the Return from Saint Cloud to Paris by Land*), which already appears in 1788, or the bizarre *Voyage pittoresque de Paris à Saint-Germain, par le chemin de fer. Narré par Madame de Trouillard, portière rue Muffetard, No. 147, bis, à Mademoiselle Bourbillon, garde-malade demeu-*

rant dans la même numéro (*The Picturesque Journey from Paris to Saint-Germain by Rail. Told by Madame de Trouillard, Doorkeeper of rue Muffetard 147, to Mademoiselle Bourbillon, a Nurse Residing at the Same Address*), which is the smallest publication in the Bibliothèque Nationale, and whose pages to this day have never been cut. It would almost seem that the accounts of room journeys were in any case a reaction to a perceived road weariness. "Already another journey! Yes, dear reader!" Alois Schreiber complains as early as 1797, only to move on in both senses of the word: "Would you like to come along? I'll take you neither to the ruins of Palmyra, nor to the pyramids or the piked pillars, as our linguists call them, nor to Mecca to see the grave of the Prophet, nor to Kaufbeueren to see the tomb of Saint Walpurgis, but rather to my quiet little room. You can stay with me, as if you were home!" (Schreiber 11).

And already by the mid-nineteenth century, explorations had brought together such an abundance of observations and information that one could gather them into a tidy little book whose title announced the contents at length: *Die Reise im Zimmer über den Erdball, oder Historisch-Geographische Beschreibung aller Länder und Völker des Erdballes, mit Rücksicht auf demselben geschichtlich vorgefallen Merkwürdigkeiten, sammt Regentenfolge eines jeden Staates. Mit einem Conspectus und einer Einleitung in die mathematische und physikalische Erdbeschreibung bevorwortet, zusammengestellt durch Wilh. Schlungs, Geograph* (*The Journey across the Globe within a Room; or, The Historical-Geographical Description of all Lands and Peoples of the Globe, with a Consideration of Their Important Historical Curiosities, including the Ruling Lineage of Each State. With a Conspectus and Introduction to the Mathematical and Physical Qualities of the Globe, Explained and with a Preface by Wilhelm Schlungs, Geographer*). In just 138 pages, Schlungs writes a "useful work" (Schlungs i) that compiles the knowledge gained from explorations and travel accounts, historical studies, and collections, as well as transcribes it in easy-to-read tables, thus making it possible to "travel across the globe inside one's room, and observe the same curious phenomena" (Schlungs v).

Travel Reading

A.L.O.F. [Auguste Le Blanc]. *Voyage sans bouger de place*. Paris, 1809.

Anon. *Neue Reise in meinem Zimmer herum*. Basel, 1798.

Anon. *Voyage dans mes poches*. No place, 1798.

Brot, J. *Voyage autour de ma cave*. No place, no year.

Des Ecores, Ch. *Expéditions autour de ma tente*. Paris, 1887.

D'Houay, S. *Voyage dans ma maison*. Rouen, 1880.

Drève, Jean. *Voyage au centre de ma chambre*. Brussels, 1957.

Fée, Antoine-Laurant-Apollinaire. *Voyage autour de ma bibliothèque*. Paris, 1856.

Gériolles, A. de, and M. Brosset. *Le Tour de Paris . . . en 280 Jours*. Paris, no year.

Heaume, Hippolyte Mazier du. *Voyage d'un jeune grec à Paris*. 2 vols. Paris, 1824.

Houssaye, Arsène. *Voyage à Venise*, in Houssaye, *Œuvres*. Vol. 4. Paris, 1855. 227–317.

Jaquet, Friedrich David. *Reise in meinem Zimmer in den Jahren 1812 und 1813*. Riga, 1813.

Jourdan, J. L. E. B. *Promenade nocturne autour de ma chambre ou les loisir du cabinet*. Paris, 1827.

Karr, Alphonse. *Histoire d'un voisin*, in Karr, *Contes et nouvelles*. Paris, 1852. 344–52.

———. *Voyage dans Paris*, in Karr, *Contes et nouvelles*. Paris, 1852. 302–44.

Linden, Adrien. *Voyage dans un tiroir*. Second edition. Paris, 1886.

Mangin, Arthur. *Voyage scientifique autour de ma chambre*. Third edition. Paris, 1889.

Néel. *Voyage de Paris à Saint-Cloud par mer, et retour de Saint-Cloud à Paris, par terre.* Paris, An VI (= 1788).

Orlan, Pierre Mac, ed. *Voyage dans Paris.* Paris, 1949.

Saglier, L., Abbé. *Voyage d'un enfant à Paris.* Paris, 1870.

Schlungs, Wilhelm. *Die Reise im Zimmer über den Erdball, oder Historisch-Geographische Beschreibung aller Länder und Völker des Erdballes.* Düsseldorf, 1842.

Schreiber, Alois. *Reise meines Vetters auf seinem Zimmer.* Bremen, 1797.

Stern, Karl. *Auch eine Reise auf meinem Zimmer.* Leipzig, 1805.

Voyage pittoresque des Paris à Saint-Germain, par le chemin de fer, Narré par Madame de Trouillard, portière rue Muffetard, No. 147, bis, à Mademoiselle Bourbillon, garde-malade demeurant dans la même numéro. No place, no year.

Framed Views

Spend a little time with me at my window: We'll saunter from
discovery to discovery, bursting with surprise after surprise.

Chaumont, 8f.

I believe in always being at my window, and yet I'm never
there. The moment I step up to it, I am gone, without quite
knowing where to.

Houssaye, 184

Man was born to travel. "Life is a journey." Even the grave is a
road to another world.

Houssaye, 172

Gaston Chaumont's *Voyage à ma fenêtre* (*Journey to My Window*)
appeared more than half a century after Xavier de Maistre traveled beyond the confines of his room without having to leave it.
Once again, another room journey, yet one different from that of
de Maistre, who never cares about gazing at the world beyond his
room; instead, Chaumont takes the world as part of his own interior space, the room playing a generally more subordinate role
with its furnishings and their various histories. The real story is
found by looking out the window and observing closely while also
simultaneously distancing oneself. One only needs to know how to

observe — otherwise, the world remains cut off and meaningless. The gaze is what brings it to life. "Oh reader, what a lovely thing is observation!" (Chaumont 12) the narrator can rightly claim, while at the same time depicting the room journey as cognitive training. Its object is no longer just the interior of the room, and the interior of the subject, both interlocked with the objects to which memories are attached, but rather the space that encloses the gaze. Chaumont proceeds differently from de Maistre in making a decidedly visual journey that has a clear frame surrounding it, namely the window. Just as with de Maistre and his room, Chaumont describes the geographic location of his window and places his view as if it were conducting an exploration. "Spend a little time with me," he tells the reader, "at the window: We'll saunter from discovery to discovery, bursting with surprise after surprise" (Chaumont 8f.). The fact that he quotes de Maistre explicitly (and also later Alphonse Karr in the same book) reveals not only an orientation toward the room journey but also its displacement. The room is no longer a closed or adequate-enough realm for experience, but rather light and bright, needing to be open for impressions and perceptions.

Through the frame of the window, perception is sharpened and transforms passing phenomena into images and narratives that are visually as well as narratively framed. A window is like a machine that produces perceptions, but also images and narratives. It's a kind of optical instrument that in many regards structures perception. The room traveler Marie O'Kennedy thus describes the window as a kind of magnifying glass that allows the observer to perceive things more sharply, more precisely, and at the same time with greater surprise. The window functions for her literally like a diorama, like an optical instrument: "A window! That's like an actual microscope, for it seems to me that it allows an entire world to be discovered in miniature" (O'Kennedy 150). And thus it's not surprising that the discovery of photography begins with the open

MA FENÊTRE

05.0 *My Window*; in Marie O'Kennedy, *Inventaire de ma chambre*, with engravings by F. Paillet, revised and augmented 3rd ed. (Paris, 1887), 148.

window. Nicéphore Niépce, who before Daguerre and Talbot developed a viable mode of photography, wrote to his brother Claude already on May 5, 1816 (thus two decades before the sensational announcement of Daguerre's discovery): "I set up the apparatus in my workroom in front of an open window across from the aviary. I took the shot by the same means that you are well familiar with, my dear friend, and I saw appear on the white paper the same section of the aviary that one could see from the window, as well as a dim image of the window frame that was less well lit than the objects outside. . . . This is just a very rough attempt, but the image of the objects was extremely small. The possibility of painting through this means and manner seemed to me as good as certain" (Niépce 17f.). One of the few surviving exposures by Niépce also shows the view from the window. When the camera obscura evolved into photography, it also involved a space that had to be lit and that was opened up to the light. The exposures by Niépce, which we know about mostly from his letters, are images that play with the movement from inside to outside, the view from the window, and therefore with both closed and open space. In the first years of photography, this motif was taken up again and again, not least of all by William Henry Fox Talbot, who experimented with diverse views from the space of a room that belong to the earliest surviving examples of photography. This led to the exposure as object as well as a metaphor for the entire process, which also has to do with the marvelous exposure to light of the camera obscura, but which in many regards has to do with a sensibility (and not least of all, paper that could be sensitized).

And yet the room is above all a place of retreat that, through the necessary restraint imposed by its *framing*, causes impressions and perceptions to be transformed into images and narratives — which the room-traveling observer points out and draws attention to for the world. In Gaston de Chaumont's account, the discovery of the window as a means to produce images and narra-

05.1 Nicéphore Niépce, *View from My Window in La Gras.*

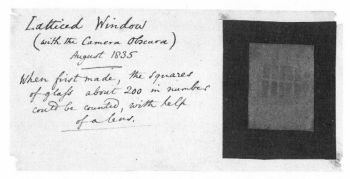

05.2 William Henry Fox Talbot, *Latticed Window Taken with the Camera Obscura*; in Anthony Burnett-Brown, *Specimens and Marvels: The Work of William Henry Fox Talbot* (Bradford, 2000), 8.

tives is consequently described as a replacement for long-distance travel. "The usual walks that we take together," so an old man tells the narrator along the way, "allow us to just take a turn around the village and have a good look around us, rather than take some trip around the world and take nothing home from it. And I know for myself as well that it's much better to spend an hour looking from a window than it is to rush around the entire village" (Chaumont 7f.). From the trip around the world to the stroll around the village, and from this to the journey of the view from a window — these are the legs of the journey that are easy to perceive as life's journey, and at whose end those who bring the most home are those who stay at home.

Also Arsène Houssaye, to whom Charles Baudelaire dedicated his *Fleurs du mal* (*Flowers of Evil*), offers at the beginning of his window journey a melancholy swan song for his trip: "I have gone to the ends of the visible and invisible world, I've seen the Venus de Milo, as well as all of ancient art. I've idolized Proudhon's figures, especially all of modern art. — I have traveled through Plato's shining spheres, the entire ancient world, as well as the modern era with Jesus Christ on the Mount of Calvary. — I have lived in all the ideal republics. I have been everywhere and even much further. I have even journeyed inside myself and seen what no other traveler has experienced, but I know myself no better as a result" (Houssaye 1). Yet such a retraction is not meant as resignation — rather the opposite: the view through the window opens up in the strictest sense of the word a new kind of journey, one that includes its own view: "Whenever I have nothing to do . . . , I open my window and journey. A journey forth from my window. Doesn't this also mean that if windows aren't opened the world is shut?" (Houssaye 7) asks Houssaye rhetorically, not only to play off of the metaphor of the world as a book, whereby one can study the view sharpened by the framing of the window all the more pointedly, but also to associate the view through the window and the enchantments of the world with love. The fundamental reason for the window journey could hardly be expressed any better: "And thus a new love is a new world — heaven and earth as one — its joy comparable to that of Christopher Columbus. But how far we've traveled!" (Houssaye 127).

The discovery of the window as a realm for visual experience has a long history that begins at the latest with E. T. A. Hoffmann's

05.3 Illustration from Arsène Houssaye, "Voyage à ma fenêtre"; in *Œuvres*, vol. 4 (Paris, 1855), 3.

05.4 Illustration from Arsène Houssaye, "Voyage à ma fenêtre"; in *Œuvres*, vol. 4 (Paris, 1855), 10.

XXXVI.

OU LE LECTEUR FERMERA MON LIVRE ET OUVRIRA SA FENÊTRE.

HISTOIRE DE L'AME.

DERNIER CHAPITRE.

. . . .
. . . .
. . . .
. . . .
. . . .
. . . .
. . . .
. . . .
. . . .
. . . .
. . . .
. . . .
. . . .
. . . .

15

05.5 Page from Arsène Houssaye, "Voyage à ma fenêtre"; in Œuvres, vol. 4 (Paris, 1855), 15.

last story, "Des Vetters Eckfenster" ("My Cousin's Corner Window"), with its exploration of storytelling and the potential for passing impressions to develop into literature. In the literature of the nineteenth century, we find the actual discovery of the framed view. Works of realism especially turn the limits of perception and the genesis of images into principles of storytelling and narrative potential. From Stifter to Raabe, from Andersen to Tolstoy, as well as unknown works by Karl Friedrich Kretschmann to Ada Christen, the window provides a way of viewing that turns it into a means of experience.

Also in painting from the nineteenth century, the window frame is a widely used *topos* that we find in countless paintings and that in turn looks back to a long tradition (such as interior scenes). The view from the window is therefore more than a simple subject among many; it also has to do with the frame that it is played off of, indeed with the implicit thematization of the limits of the image by the frame that first helps it become an image. Within the picture frame a second frame is introduced which, set back within the visual space, delineates the borders of what it enables us to see. This thematization of the excerpt as a *conditio sine qua non* of the generation of images from phenomena can result in a very complex play of changing views, as shown in a painting by Karl Friedrich Göser, which also implicates the viewer. On the one hand, he is supposed to follow the path of his gaze and make discoveries — even when these can only be found within the static space of the picture and not in the almost cinematic space of the framed view of the world: "This naïve peep show of Biedermeier life was, with its *whir-whir — next image*, the so-called cinema of our grandfathers" (Heilborn 90). Yet even if the film of the window journey simply runs on and never ends, the journey must still end somehow. "This journey has neither a beginning nor an end. Nor indeed must it last forever" (Houssaye 221). And thus the narrator in Houssaye's book closes the frame, established with Tony Johannot's frontis-

05.6 Karl Friedrich Göser, *Self-Portrait in the Studio*, 1835; in Sabine Schulze, ed., *Innenleben: Die Kunst des Intérieurs; Vermeer bis Kabakov* (Ostfildern-Ruit, 1998), 123.

piece, with which the book ends and simultaneously a new window opens through which the viewer and the reader can travel. The empty page which we found earlier in de Maistre's *Voyage autour de ma chambre* is now here an empty chapter in which the reader shuts the book and—ideally—opens his window (Houssaye 225).

* * *

An addendum: in the short story "The Traveler's Story of a Terribly Strange Bed" by Wilkie Collins, the window frame, as well as Xavier de Maistre's *Voyage autour de ma chambre*, saves the narrator from a gruesome death. And at the same time, it all has to do with a run of good luck: during a visit to Paris, the narrator had won so much money in a casino that it had to declare bankruptcy. Yet where could one go with all that cash in a strange city in the middle of the night? Meanwhile, a number of false friends soon turn up with whom he drinks champagne and who make clear that he can no longer walk through the city, but instead must remain in the building to avoid danger. Yet as he lies in a room in a large bed, he feels himself in danger and, despite there being nothing to read, thinks back to de Maistre's book: "While my eyes wandered from wall to wall, a remembrance of de Maistre's delightful little book, *Voyage autour de ma chambre*, occurred to me. I resolved to imitate the French author, and find occupation and amusement enough to relieve the tedium of wakefulness, by speaking a mental inventory of every article of furniture I could see, and by following up to their sources the multitude of associations that even a chair, a table, or a wash-hand stand may be made to call forth. In the nervous unsettled state of my mind at that moment, I found it much easier to make my inventory than to make my reflections, and thereupon soon gave up all hope of thinking in de Maistre's fanciful track—or, indeed, of thinking at all" (Collins 36). With his perceptions thus sharpened to such an extent, he looks more closely at an image that is painted on the wooden headboard of his bed: depicted there is a man with a feather hat who has placed a hand above his eyes and is looking up. Yet slowly his hat and then his head disappear from the frame, for the bed's canopy, the narrator realizes, is about to fall on his head and suffocate him. He escapes through the window and saves his own life.

Travel Reading

Brüggemann, Heinz. *"Aber schickt keinen Poeten nach London!" Großstadt und literarische Wahrnehmung im 18. und 19. Jahrhundert: Texte und Interpretationen.* Reinbek bei Hamburg, 1985.

Chaumont, Gaston de. *Voyage à ma fenêtre*. Paris, 1865.

Christen, Ada. *Jungfer Mutter*. Dresden, 1892.

Collins, Wilkie. "The Traveler's Story of a Terribly Strange Bed." In *After Dark*. London, 1925. 29–43 (First published in *Household Words*.)

Duro, Paul, ed. *The Rhetoric of the Frame: Essays on the Boundaries of the Artwork*. Cambridge, 1996.

Heilborn, Adolf. *Die Reise durchs Zimmer*. Berlin, 1924.

Hoffmann, E. T. A. "Des Vetters Eckfenster." In *Späte Werke*. Munich, 1965. 595–622 (First published, Berlin, 1822.)

Houssaye, Arsène. "Voyage à ma fenêtre." In Houssaye, *Œuvres*. Vol. 4. Paris, 1855. 1–225.

Kretschmann, Karl Friedrich. "Scarron am Fenster." In W. G. Becker, ed., *Taschenbuch zum geselligen Vergnügen*. Leipzig, 1798. 47–67.

Langen, August. *Anschauungsformen in der deutschen Dichtung des 18. Jahrhunderts: Rahmenschau und Rationalismus*. Darmstadt, 1968 (First published 1931/32.)

Mesureur, Mme. "Voyage autour d'une fenêtre." In Mesureur, *Les Châtaignes, suivi de Voyage autour d'une fenêtre et de Au bord de la Durolle*. Paris, 1895. 41–62.

Niépce, Nicéphore. *Der Blick aus dem Fenster: Gesammelte Briefe (1816–1828)*. Hamburg, 1998.

O'Kennedy, Marie. *Inventaire de ma chambre*. Third edition. Paris, 1887. (First edition, Paris, 1884.)

Schultze, Sabine, ed. *Innenleben: Die Kunst des Intérieurs; Vermeer bis Kabakov*. Ostfildern-Ruit, 1998.

Starl, Timm. "Fenster." *Kritik der Fotografie*. http://www.kritik-der -fotografie.at/12-Fenster.htm.

The Life of Plants

I have ever found my greatest happiness in a garden over which I could have jumped — in a chamber in which I could not take three paces.

Karr, 69

Sit down and travel.

Karr, 56

Perhaps it has something to do with the immobility of plants that they play such a special role for this form of travel, or perhaps with the fact that, despite their inability to move, they change and are subject to the seasons, and sometimes come from far-off places to which they occasionally bear witness. More than a few travel texts from the nineteenth century and early twentieth century limit themselves to the realm of the garden and the plant life of a building, and in many of them plants play an important role. The two most important texts from the nineteenth century are arguably Alphonse Karr's *Voyage autour de mon jardin* (*A Tour round My Garden*), which appeared in 1845 and was even turned into a play that premiered at the Comédie Française under the title *Roses jaunes* (*Yellow Roses*) (Virlogeux iv), and Georges Aston's *L'ami Kips: Voyage d'un botaniste dans sa maison* (*Friend Kips: A Botanist's Journey through His House*) from 1879. In the latter work, the journey through the plant world of an apartment building is a virtual story of initiation in which the protagonist reveals the dark history of the would-be, as well as the odd botanist Kips, and becomes his son-in-law at the end. More precisely, it concerns itself with three journeys through the building, which lies in the middle of Paris. The first leads him to the cellar, the second into the inner yard, and the third over the building's façade, which is explored, floor by floor, balcony by balcony, and plant by plant. The first reveals the light amid the darkness, the second the struggle for survival, and the third finally the "fonctions de relations dans le règne végétal" (the function of relations in the plant realm), and through them the laws of relations of life in general. *Per flora ad astra* — and right in the middle of Paris.

The narrator Georges Nédon's main concern is to classify and label the plant collection of his uncle Horace Nédon, a famous scientist who is also a member of the Academy.* The order of plants also describes the order of life. Yet one day, a man named Kips shows up who lives in the building and who regards the narrator in intense and peculiar fashion, sharing with him a secret that for the first time implies that social life in general is chaotic: "Having closely observed the plants, I have ferreted out a number of secrets, discovering things that others have not noted or did not want to believe" (Aston 6). Thus there is a secret life to plants, something that a few years ago David Attenborough's prizewinning

---

* How does one describe the room of an academic such as this? Just so: "Uncle Horace sits comfortably in his chair at his desk, his feet in a foot warmer no matter the season. To his left sits a stack of blue and pink brochures on which is written: *Scientific Work, Reports to the Academy of Sciences.* To his right are several copies of the *London Journal of Botany* and the *Annals of Natural Science.* Before him on the desk sits a piece of glazed paper, a bit further off the antique inkwell, next to which stands a little bottle of phosphorus in which one dips matches. In the large metal shell lie styluses, pocketknives, goose feathers, a collection of penknives, gum resin, glue, sandarac, mostly the old cleaning implements that used to be so common" (Aston 71).

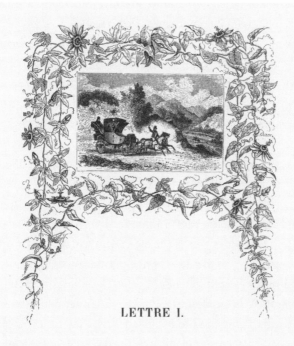

LETTRE I.

Vous souvient-il, mon ami, du jour où vous partites pour ce long et beau voyage dont les préparatifs vous occupaient depuis si longtemps?

J'arrivai le matin pour passer quelques instants avec vous, ainsi que j'en avais l'habitude ; — j'ignorais que ce jour fût celui de votre départ, et je restai surpris de l'air inusité qu'avait votre maison ; — tout le monde paraissait inquiet et affairé ; — vos domestiques montaient et descendaient rapidement. Une élégante

06.0 Page from Alphonse Karr, *Voyage autour de mon jardin*, vol. 2 (Paris, 1845), 1.

The Private Life of Plants invoked in its title. Despite their relative stasis, plants are also alive, and are highly sensitive. Kips wants — of course secretly — to initiate Georges into the mysteries of the secret life of plants, and to this end to leave the apartment building early one morning with him in order, so he claims, to travel to the country. Yet how, then, will he be back by 8 a.m. in order to catalog his uncle's plants? The journey in fact doesn't pass through the countryside, but rather into the depths of the building, because, according to Kips: "It is not necessary to go far away in order to find the thousand different types of plant life. To limit oneself to a small space, but in the most thorough manner possible to study in detail whatever phenomena you come across is the best way and means to enter upon a serious and solid education. . . . Whatever is taught with sound methods will not be forgotten. We walk through the entire building in accordance with 'Nature's inherent order,' as your uncle would say in his teachings. We begin in the cellar and end up on the roof" (Aston 18f.).

A building provides enough space in which to study and understand the secret life of plants — even if it's one found within a large city. And in the end, a journey through a building, through the *Flora domestica*, is enough to allow one to understand the secret life of its inhabitants and to establish a new order. The order of nature becomes the order of culture, the laws of plants a standard for human society. But in turn, human beings assign plants their own form and identity, and thus the description of plants is, to put it mildly, anthropomorphic. Thus the first journey through the building enters the cellar and the realm of mushrooms, through which one immediately learns that among people, as with plants, there are two different categories: "plain types and murderers" (Aston 21). Mushrooms belong indeed to the second category. They are, so it actually says later on, vampires. Yet these vampires can actually light up in the dark, as they are phosphorescent. And whenever the muscles of the mushroom spores are experimentally innervated under a microscope that is brought along, the mushrooms look like stars — botanical lights in the darkness of the cellar that are no less marvelous than the stars above. What's more, they are lights that demonstrate a form of sensitivity that goes far beyond the pure exposure to light.

In the cellar there is also a torture chamber. It is secured with a lock that uses the password "KNIGHT," the name of a famous British scholar. The torture chamber is in truth a fully outfitted laboratory. There plants are examined — and in fact tortured . . . they suffer from chlorosis or "albinisme héréditaire" ("hereditary albinism") (Aston 44). The choice of password is therefore no accident, for Knight indeed worked with positive as well as negative geotropism and heliotropism. It has nothing to do with dryness or dampness, light or darkness, or the force of gravity alone, as is often thought, whereby the plants align themselves according to either the sun or gravity. The uncle searches for a "suitable relation" between these elements. However, Kips thinks that this cannot be found and observed through experimentation, "because it is not possible for human beings to artificially reproduce the precise conditions of nature" (Aston 55). Indeed, why do leaves and stems grow upward and roots downward? That is one of the unsolved questions of the secret life of plants, which is no less complex than human existence. The journey through the floral world of the cellar leads to basic questions of existence. Similar to this is the second journey, the one that leads to the plants one finds between cobblestones. They interest Kips — who obviously has read Darwin — because of the continual struggle to survive that they must make, and also because many of the plants have migrated. Survival and migration — these are the secrets of the life of plants in a Parisian courtyard. Meanwhile, a third and last journey begins on the roof, from which it rappels downward floor by floor as it explores the plant world of the balconies before ending with a discussion of carnivorous plants and new hypotheses about sundews (Aston 224f.). Once the secrets of the life of plants are solved, so too are those of the ones who discover them: Kips, it turns out, is really named de Corbelles and was not a botanist but rather a physicist. He lost his daughter, whose husband absconded with his granddaughter, and he has traveled about the world in vain while in search of the latter. But at last the family is brought together as a result of the journey through the building, which also holds a place for the narrator as a future son-in-law.

Such a narrative integration within the genealogical tree is not found in Alphonse Karr. His *Voyage autour de mon jardin* (*A Tour round My Garden*) describes in two volumes and nearly seven hundred pages nothing more, but also nothing less, than his garden. This — but not the person — displays the intensity and the rhythm of an adventure in and of itself. It is an herbarium, a kitchen garden, and at the same time an imaginary mythological realm. Karr is one of the bourgeois eccentrics of nineteenth-century French literature. In 1829, he rented a very small house on the hill of Montmarte that was really just one room, but had a garden in which there was even a small grotto with a fountain. He lived in this little house with his monkey, Emmanuel. He spent the day in his garden, and then met up with his friend Léon Gatayes in the evening to walk to Saint-Ouen and swim there for some hours together. Later, Karr lived on the rue Vivienne, right next to the Bibliothèque Nationale, and there he set up, as with his later apartment on the rue de la Tour d'Auvergne, a garden on the terrace of his seventh-floor apartment. Despite living in the middle of Paris, he didn't like the idea of living without a garden. His apartment, as Walter Benjamin notes in *The Arcades Project*, is highly unusual: "The apartment is hung in black; he has windowpanes of violet and white frosted glass. He has neither tables nor chairs . . . , and he sleeps on a divan — fully dressed, I'm told, . . . and writes sitting on the floor. . . . His walls are decorated with various old things" (Benjamin 223). Nor can such a scene be without a domestic, a "mulatto" (ibid.) in Oriental dress. In the middle of Paris, Karr sets up an apartment that looks more like the Orient than the Palais Royal, which lies just around the corner. And his garden ends up meaning more to him than a substitute for a journey — it becomes an entire world. "Travelers," he complains, "are strange beings who go to great distances, and at great expense, to see new things, without having taken the trouble to look at their feet or over their heads, where as many extraordinary and unknown things are passing as they can possibly desire to know" (Karr 8). Karr's journey through the garden develops more as a close analogy to, rather than replacing the journey of, a friend who wanders around and through the world, now and then sending back a report from Peru or some other distant place, and then at the end of the story appearing out of nowhere after many weeks, disillusioned and exhausted, with the well-rested Karr meanwhile feeling as if he has hardly completed half his journey through his garden — so multifarious are the discoveries that he has made there already (Karr 332).

If we wanted to appreciate Karr's many detailed descriptions and observations, we could speak of four discoveries that appear continually in his text in modified forms: the discovery of the evidence of facticity, inverse order, the universal links between all things, and finally the necessity and naturalness of travel.

While the one who journeys far away can bring home accounts of distant lands that hardly anyone can believe, and that only become powerful in their ability to subvert the everyday, the one who journeys through a room or garden can rely on firsthand evidence. If the subject is plants, there is nothing in the account that can be doubted. The far-off is the place of the fictional, but the near-at-hand is that of the fact. Travelers claim to have seen the Cyclops. Those who travel their rooms, however, describe spiders as Cyclops — and have evidence on their side. And even the far-off already lies nearby: "I go down three steps. Here we are in China!" (Karr 18) — wisteria indeed being from China and bringing the far near as a result. The same is true for works of art in far-off museums, which distance can sometimes make difficult to see, but which can be seen in dissimilar, yet even more beautiful form right at home. When Karr looks out his window, he sees an Ostade, a Ruysdael, etc., and doesn't have to pay 9,950 francs for a still life

06.1 Illustration from Alphonse Karr, *Voyage autour de mon jardin*, vol. 2 (Paris, 1845), 73.

depicting a bouquet of flowers that cost only 20 francs. The garden easily levels the playing field in regard to the value of works of art. It's a place of aesthetic, theoretical, and metaphysical discoveries: through the mode of the journey, the human world suddenly appears in other terms. The order of things is turned around. Karr perhaps sees continuity in the natural laws and behavioral patterns within the human realm, but really curious incidents among the flowers and insects. And here the journey also plays an important role, and reveals through closer attention that insects also travel, though not all of them in the same manner. A gall wasp takes almost five months to travel across a leaf that is no bigger than a sixpence (Karr 208), while migratory birds travel great distances. Each leaf, each plant is its own world, with its own inhabitants and its own itineraries. And when a leaf or a flower dies, so does an entire world and its inhabitants. So at a minimum, Karr's imagined world seeks to perpetuate creation in the garden, and also needs destruction to accomplish that. As an observer, Karr is a new creator of world order.

Not the distant, not the city, but rather the garden holds ready the flow of impressions that later modernity rings in: "See how everything passes before you; see how everything travels to show you new objects" (Karr 58). Everything is in motion—that is the observation of the room traveler. Alphonse Karr thus compares the view of his garden to that of a moving wagon.[†] "It appears to me that I am the sport of an illusion similar to that which we experience in a wagon or a boat, when I see the flowers appear, each in its turn, around me; it would appear, in fact, that I changed my place" (Karr 55).

In the middle of this reversal, in which the transitory becomes the constant and the constant the transitory, the law of relations becomes apparent: "Great and small are only such with relation to ourselves" (Karr 29). When even insects cross what for them are huge distances, and the microscope reveals ever newer ways of traveling, what does it mean, then, to cross larger or smaller distances on a globe that is only one planet among thousands, just like grains of sand on a beach? For the room traveler, the micro- and macrocosm are interchangeable. Thus, as in the story of the prince who holds a walnut, inside of which is a hazelnut, inside of which there is another nut, and so on, until from the last nut a huge picture unfolds, Karr folds up his world in order to unfold it again. What also becomes apparent amid this game is the law that lies beneath all journeys. Travel becomes a transitory principle, an obvious law of both nature and culture. The seasons themselves are in motion, and travelers visit nothing but seasons. And in the middle of this world of conversion and transformation, what is played out anew day after day is the mystery of creation: "We have it in our power to enjoy the most solemn and magnificent spectacle—the creation of the world!" (Karr 59).

[†] Karr also describes his own perception in this way: "After we have viewed small things closely and attentively, we gradually lose the feeling of their dimensions; this green moss appears to me to be trees, and the insects which wander over its velvet surface, assume in my eyes an importance equal to the deer and stags of a park" (Karr 86).

Karr's journey through his garden is the story of the reenchantment of the world—almost like in a children's story. Georges d'Albrays's *Voyages autour de mon jardin* (*Journeys around My Garden*) nearly a half a century later also tells such a children's story of an inhabited world, in which butterflies resemble little elves and are able to talk to one another and mutually warn each other of danger, in which ants are the real workers of the world, and bees are nature's chefs. And at the end, the sparrow sings nature's message: "Among it and in the circle of the family one is better off than anywhere else" (d'Albrays 47).

Yet Karr's journey is also representative of a broader botanical literature that pursues such reenchantment in other ways—such as with Carl Müller, whose programmatic book, with its wonderful three-part title *Das Buch der Pflanzenwelt: Reise um die Welt; Versuch einer kosmischen Botanik* (*The Book of the Plant World: Journey around the World; In Search of a Cosmic Botany*), in this regard "sees the plant world to some extent as a microcosm, as the world in miniature" (Müller vi and index, 886). Behind the journey around the world in Müller's book is clearly the first part of a room journey (and one review noted this) that does not just need the space of a room, but instead seeks to conceive of the entire world in a single plant. Such journeys show up toward the end of the nineteenth century and the beginning of the twentieth in numerous botanical and popular science books. When R. H. Francé and Ernst Fuhrmann talk about the world of plants, they do so with Karl Blossfeldt's photographic works, which were published as microphotography in his famous volumes *Wundergarten der Natur* (*Nature's Garden of Wonders*) and *Urformen der Kunst* (*Primary Forms of Art*), and which in one fell swoop made him one of the leaders in new directions in photography. One of his admirers was Walter Benjamin, who in his review of Blossfeldt describes the reading of his books as a journey: "We, the observers, wander amid these giant plants like Liliputians" (Benjamin, "The News

06.2 View of the Hall of Palms, Hannover, 1882; in Georg Kohlmaier and Barna von Sartory, *Das Glashaus ein Bautyp des 19. Jahrhunderts* (Munich, 1981), 621.

06.3 Interior view of the Hall of Plants, Paris, 1898; in Georg Kohlmaier and Barna von Sartory, *Das Glashaus ein Bautyp des 19. Jahrhunderts* (Munich, 1981), 708.

about Flowers," 157). An almost surreal transformation found in the early comic *Little Nemo in Slumberland*, published by Winsor McCay between 1905 and 1911, is the dreamlike sequence of images, through which the protagonists sometimes wander among mushrooms as if lost in a dream, though at the same time remaining highly alert to all that's around them. Yet it is reserved for the photographer Albert Renger-Patzsch to describe this visual explora-

06.4.1, 06.4.2 Illustrations from Winsor McCay, *Little Nemo in Slumberland*, originally published in the *New York Herald* on October 22, 1905.

tion in words: "What is delightful is that through photography we are forced to focus our eyes on the more or less small organisms that blossom, such that in a sense we are forced to see through the eyes of an insect and make their world our own. Only through the intense observation of the blossoms looked at so closely and in detail are we granted a view into a world of fantastic beauty. We marvel at the extreme perfection of its structure and the final culmination of form and color. We recognize the formal elements from which the style of a particular people grows, and we sense statistical laws that are so stable that they are incapable of being

understood intellectually and cannot be expressed numerically"
(Renger-Patzsch 104).

Travel Reading

Anon. Review of Müller's *Buch der Pflanzenwelt. Österreichische Botanische Zeitschrift.* 1858. 35–38.

Aston, Georges. *L'ami Kips: Voyage d'un botaniste dans sa maison.* Paris, 1879.

Attenborough, David. *The Private Life of Plants.* Documentary. UK, 1995.

Benjamin, Walter. *The Arcades Project.* Trans. Howard Eiland and Kevin McLaughlin. Cambridge, 1999.

———. "News about Flowers." In *Selected Writings*, vol. 2. Trans. Michael Jennings. Cambridge, 1996. 155–57.

Blossfeldt, Karl. *Urformen der Kunst.* Berlin, 1928.

d'Albrays, Georges. *Voyages autour de mon jardin.* Paris, 1900.

Karr, Alphonse. *A Tour round My Garden.* Trans. Rev. S. G. Wood. London, 1845.

McCay, Winsor. *Little Nemo in Slumberland.* Palo Alto, CA, 2005. (First published 1905–11 in *New York Herald*.)

Müller, Carl. *Das Buch der Pflanzenwelt: Reise um die Welt; Versuch einer kosmischen Botanik.* 2 vols. Leipzig, 1857.

———. Self-published notice of his book. *Botanische Zeitung*, 1856. 885–87.

Renger-Patzsch, Albert. "Das Photographieren von Blüten." In *Deutscher Kamera Almanach: Ein Jahrbuch für die Photographie unserer Zeit.* Vol. 15. Berlin, 1924. 104–12.

Virlogeux, Louis. "Présentation." In Alphonse Karr, *Voyage autour de mon jardin.* Reprint of the Paris edition, 1851. Paris, 1979. i–xvi.

The Life of Objects

Then I turned my gaze toward the things inside my room and found myself too rich to die.

Jourdan, 96

Everything there is familiar to you, everything has a history, and for the most part it's also a part of your history. In your room you belong to yourself, you are yourself, without all the trappings of convention that you don against the outside world. . . . More often than not, doesn't a room tell us more often than not more about the character of its inhabitant than his clothes or his face?

Heilborn, 19f.

"One need only study with due exactitude the physiognomy of the homes of great collectors," writes Walter Benjamin in *The Arcades Project*. "Then one would have the key to the nineteenth-century interior. Just as in the former case the objects gradually take possession of the residence, so in the latter it is a piece of furniture that would retrieve and assemble the stylistic traces of the centuries" (Benjamin 218). One of the truly unique books of nineteenth-century literature, which appeared in 1881 in two handsome volumes, is by one of these great collectors: Edmond de Goncourt's *La maison d'un artiste* (*The House of an Artist*). In no less than 739 pages, the book lists in minute detail the objects that can be found

07.0 The Goncourts' home in Auteuil; in Edmond and Jules Goncourt; *Blitzlichter: Portraits aus dem 19. Jahrhundert* (Nördlingen, 1989), no page.

inside his house. The two volumes are nothing other than a description of things and their history, and now and then how some came to be purchased. There are art objects, furniture, drawings, porcelain, paintings, books, manuscripts, *japonaiserie* and other things from Asia, rare books and other notable *bibelots*. The gaze that describes it all wanders from room to room, without ignoring the garden and the contents of drawers. It employs a form of ekphrasis through the use of dense lists that vivify the objects, and in the description of them seeks to detail its own story, behind which the story of its owner retreats. The objects form the story of the inhabitant, who seeks to take his story from the description drawn from the viewing of them. Thus the house is neither a museum nor an archive or a special collection: it is in part all of these and above all a space in which objects take on a life of their own, and the life of the inhabitant is manifested as our gaze travels through the thickly woven surfaces of things.

Edmond de Goncourt supplied his book with a brief foreword that consists of a single sentence. He asks in his house in Auteuil on June 26, 1880: "Why does no one not write a treatise about objects during times in which objects, whose subtle melancholy the Latin poet spoke of, are so strongly connected to the literary description of human history, and among which human existence meanders on?"

In the nineteenth century, this association of description and history, according to Goncourt, grants objects in programmatic fashion their privileged condition. This change in the relation to things marks a historic turning point that occurred between the eighteenth and nineteenth centuries, characterized by a new accentuation of life. The eighteenth century was still concerned with "external life." One's own house was nothing more than a space in which one slept, life taking place elsewhere. In the nineteenth century, however, the house becomes more than a place of retreat: one leads a "sedentary life next to the fireplace" (Goncourt 2) amid supposedly inanimate objects, which virtually now were turned into objects of desire. The wife, so states Goncourt, no longer seeks to fulfill her husband's fancy at home, for objects fill this gap. The same is true for room travel, which also achieves another status.

A further example from the history of room travel that supports Goncourt's thesis with respect to the eighteenth century is the idea of the room journey as a journey that, in a certain sense, revolves around the sorely missed wife. In Louis-François-Marie Bellin de La Liborlière's *Voyage dans le boudoir de Pauline* (*A Journey around Pauline's Boudoir*), which appeared in the very year that marks the beginning of the nineteenth century, we find a quote from Jean-Jacques Rousseau's *Nouvelle Heloïse* (*New Heloise*) used as a motto that sums up the room journey as one of pleasure in both senses:

07.1 The Goncourts' home in Auteuil; in Edmond and Jules Goncourt; *Blitzlichter: Portraits aus dem 19. Jahrhundert* (Nördlingen, 1989), no page.

"Here I am in your workroom, in the sanctuary which above all my heart worships. . . . How enchanted is this secret visit! . . . Everything here nourishes the desire that consumes me! . . . Oh Julie! You are everywhere!" The beloved Pauline has left behind nineteen years' worth of one thousand "charmes," all of which still hold traces of her: "Let us journey through this wonderful room, where I still find her in every step I take, in every object I encounter and which beckons my gaze. Alas! Never shall a journey have been more picturesque, yet at the same time more single-minded, as is this one for me" (Bellin de La Liborlière 10f.). What pervades the journey around the room is the expectation of meeting her, thus making it in a sense a "sentimental journey" whose route is determined by one's feelings, the choice of objects, and how they are observed. The gaze wanders from object to object and yet sees

07.2 The Goncourts' "attic" in Auteuil; in Edmond and Jules Goncourt, *Journal: Mémoires de la vie littéraire*, vol. 3 (Paris, 1989), illustrated page 16.

nothing but the absent/present Pauline, moving from the mirror to the bell, from the grandfather's clock to the harp, from the fan to her wig and her shoes, from the tea table to the ottoman to the writing desk, wandering finally to the bookshelves. "Captivated by the objects that surround me, I have no desire to discover others" (Bellin de La Liborlière 107).

* * *

For Edmond de Goncourt, however, just over a half century later, women have disappeared, and in the end his passion is for those things that in fact serve to erase the memory of the beloved. This is also true of Goncourt's brother, Jules, with whom he had written all his books and collected all his objects, and who had died ten years earlier, though not before suffusing the house with his presence in the form of the collection itself. And so Edmond renovated the house in order that all the objects could have a suitable place, emptying Jules's room in the process. The description of the life of these objects is at the same time the effort to exorcise Jules's ghost so as to bury him once and for all.

For Goncourt, this passion for objects is more than a personal passion: it is a sign of the times, indeed a contemporary form of its sensibility. The *bricbracomanie*, which in the eighteenth century was still a passion of older men, is now the passion of an entire generation, an almost libidinous passion: the present is represented by a "nearly human tenderness for things" (Goncourt 3). It is a solitary pleasure, lying somewhere between boredom and uncertainty about the future, whereby amid objects one can glimpse history, life, and also what can be handed down to the future. Objects are more than just possessions: they are women and children, history and desire, memories and happiness. They come from countries all over the world and allow access to multifaceted stories and interpretations. They invite stories, but also further travels. The interiority that, according to Goncourt, the nineteenth century discovered and formulated in theory and in practice is in no way that of the subject, but rather that of the home, in which the objects lead their own life, and yet seek to be brought to life by the gaze of the observer: the interiority of the nineteenth century is the interior of the home, the world of objects that attract the gaze. Subjectivity achieves its shape, life, and history in the mirror of objects, and first finds its own place in the space of the room or the house.

Just three years earlier, Goncourt published *Voyage dans un grenier* (*Journey around the Attic*), which in its passage through his house in many ways ends up akin to it, presenting selected objects from the collection in four-color reproductions or facsimiles as well as supplying catalogs and inventories, and featuring collections of autographs and first editions. And in 1884, Marie O'Kennedy published her *Inventaire de ma chambre* (*An Inventory of My Room*), much of which constitutes a poetic litany. Thus the legs of her journey read as she reviews the objects that surround her: "My crucifix . . . , my bed . . . , my desk . . . , my sewing box . . . , my mir-

07.3 Edmond de Goncourt; in Edmond and Jules Goncourt, *Journal: Mémoires de la vie littéraire*, vol. 3 (Paris, 1989), llustrated page 14.

ror . . . , my piano . . . , my window . . . , my bookshelf . . . , my clock . . . , my flowerbox . . . , my birdcage . . . , my wardrobe . . . , my little font of holy water" (O'Kennedy 284). As she states, "I have looked at, studied, questioned nearly everything that belongs to me in the little space of my home, and everything has responded and given me something" (O'Kennedy 283). And so, it's possible to surmise, even the walls began to talk. Objects live, speak, teach, and give pleasure.

This singular development of the "long century" continues in many surprising ways to modern times, though we might have expected the "transcendental homelessness" of the interior of the home to have long since lost its enchantment — and yet not at all: as late as 1924, Adolf Heilborn outlines in his *Die Reise durchs Zimmer* (*The Journey through the Room*) a "cultural history of the residence and its furnishings" (Heilborn 5), and leads the reader into "far reaches he has never before seen." "We will travel through many countries and eras, and you can just sit quietly in your chair or just remain lying on your sofa. I want to take you to the one place that, of all the places on Earth, you know the least of all. Your room!" (Heilborn 9). "The room is," according to Heilborn, "the least familiar place in the world. In darkest Africa, at the far poles, and in hidden Tibet, we are more in the know than we are in our own room" (Heilborn 10). The room is thus a spatial embodiment of individual and collective histories, carrying with it traces of human development and its desire for dwelling *and* the individual touch of the inhabitant; consequently, it can be interpreted as an apparent integration of the micro- and the macrocosm. It's a protective space of one's individuality and an embodiment of one's history *and* the perceivable materialization of a collective cultural development, which Heilborn sketches out in diverse forays: "Everything inside is familiar to you, everything has a history, and for the most part it's a part of *your* history. In your room you belong to yourself, you are yourself, without all the trappings of convention that you don against the outside world" (Heilborn 9). Therefore it's about, among other things, the chair, the fireplace, the carpet, and the window, but also the meal, the Christmas tree, and the houseplants. The bourgeois interior turns into an interior world that is enriched with the history of the inhabitant and likewise with the history of human development. Both leave traces here that are revealed through the room journey.

Travel Reading

Benjamin, Walter. *The Arcades Project*. Trans. Howard Eiland and Kevin McLaughlin. Cambridge, 1999.

C.[ousin], Charles. *Voyage dans un grenier*. Paris, 1878.

Goncourt, Edmond de. *La maison d'un artiste*. 2 vols. Paris, 1881.

Heilborn, Adolf. *Die Reise durchs Zimmer*. Berlin, 1924.

Hessel, Franz. "Vorschule des Journalismus, Ein Pariser Tagebuch."
In *Sämtliche Werke*. Vol. 2. Oldenburg, 1999. 292–329. (First
published in *Nachfeier*, Berlin, 1929.)

Jourdan, J. L. E. B. *Promenade nocturne autour de ma chambre ou
les loisir du cabinet*. Paris, 1827.

La Liborlière, Louis-François-Marie Bellin de. *Voyage dans le boudoir de Pauline*. Paris, 1800.

O'Kennedy, Marie. *Inventaire de ma chambre*. Third edition. Paris,
1887 (first edition, Paris, 1884).

Sicotte, Geneviève. "La maison texte de Goncourt." *Image & Narrative: Online Magazine of the Visual Narrative*. February 2006.
http://www.imageandnarrative.be/house_text_museum
/sicotte.htm.

The Journey through
a Sea of Images

Our century is marked by a passion for travel, and this
passion becomes every day more prevalent and intense. It is a
powerful, all-encompassing movement. Switzerland, Germany,
England, France, really all countries worth seeing and
exploring, are continuously overrun by throngs of travelers
eager to take in everything: here the wonders of nature,
there the monuments from the Middle Ages, further on the
advancement in the arts, or the endless variety of the manners
and customs of the people.

> Forster, 1f.

There were once seven stars that together were called The
Seven Sisters. Now there are only six.—Where did the seventh
one go?

> Johannot, de Musset, and Stahl, *Voyage où il vous plaira*, 28

Léon Forster's *Voyages au coin du feu* (*Fireside Travels*), which by
1850 had already appeared in its third edition, sketched out a scenario of acceleration whereby, according to him, if the dizzying
pace of travel were to continue, it would not be long before every
country would be turned into a province, Europe would become a
single country, and one would be able to easily circle the globe in
a few months, globalization thus becoming an effect of the rage for
tourism. However, what amounted geographically to the gradual
shrinking of the Earth had indeed already been put into practice

in literature. Picking up Forster's *Fireside Travels* promised breakfast in Siberia and dinner in Labrador, after which one could spend the night at sea, but without having to forsake Mother's goodnight kiss. "Hoist sail!" thus Forster called. "Off we go! The lamp is lit, a fire crackles in the fireplace, our doors are locked tight, our feet are warm, we are sunk deep within our chairs. . . . Let's open our book and bon voyage!" (Forster 6).

Such armchair journeys amid the comforts of home spread far and wide in the nineteenth century and appeared in countless variations. Most such volumes started with a picture that allowed one to view the various situations described, be they a wedding ceremony in China, the lives of elephants and apes, the history of the Incas and the Bengalis, a visit to Tenerife or Spitzbergen. Pictures were therefore essential, the new means of technical reproduction of the nineteenth century thus playing a decisive role in the literary market. In serialized novels, not only would the text appear in installments—these would also quite often be accompanied by illustrations to enhance sales and reach a wider public. And if the first edition of a novel was not illustrated, in all likelihood a second or several later editions would be. Some particularly popular texts were often engraved by more than one artist to win new readers for the same novel. And if one were interested in something in particular, as August Schilling promises in his book, "the nontraveler, who amid the quiet of his little room wishes to make a little room journey into fantasy, could especially do so with a little book in hand that provides, amid such a comfortable journey, unmistakable observations in a manner more poetic than statistical, and which elicit more pleasant rather than scientific reflections" (Schilling x).

Many such volumes appeared in France in the series brought out by Pierre-Jules Hetzel, Magasin d'Éducation et de Récréation, which ran from 1864 to 1905. Hetzel, the publisher who under the pseudonym P. J. Stahl also illustrated some of these books personally, was one of the most important publishers of the nineteenth century. In particular, the novels of Jules Verne—also published by him in the series billed as Voyages Extraordinaire—were not only immensely successful, but even today are sought-after collector's items, not least because of the lavish and numerous illustrations, which had to be a part of any fine edition. Sometimes these books were regular picture books that established a new relationship between text and image. Often the text appeared as an "illustration" of the abundant images—and not the other way around. Rodolphe Toepffer's *Voyages en zigzag* (*Zigzag Journeys*) was also a part of the publishing program, whose first title was J. J. Grandville's *Scènes de la vie privée et publique des animaux* (*Scenes from the Public and Private Life of Animals*). Because Hetzel didn't have the financing to publish it as a book, it first appeared in separate installments whose success then made possible a complete edition. It was also Hetzel who brought together Tony Johannot, one of the most important book illustrators of his time, and the romantic writer Alfred de Musset. Together they conceived of and designed the book *Voyage où il vous plaira* (*Travel Where You Please*). This was one of the first albums that even in its narrative could rightly be described as an "album," even though it is as much about "what's shown as what's written" or at the very least is a preconceived expansion of the text through images. Reading it involved a journey through a sea of images that set in motion the reader's journey. "It's about getting away, so let's get away!" cries the narrator (Johannot 4). And away you went into the realm of images.

In Goethe's *Werther*, there is a famous letter in which Werther and Lotte's spiritual kinship is articulated not only in the subtle arrangement of the scene, which harks back to literary predecessors ranging from Salomon Geßner to Jean-Jacques Rousseau, but also by Lotte's cry of "Klopstock!" The allusions to various depictions of intimacy in literary texts could not be more pointedly made. The *Voyage où il vous plaira* is also served by the rich trove of images existing in the literary tradition, and it quotes, among others, Cook, *The Wandering Jew*, Burton, and even Xavier de Maistre. All these quotes then enable the construction of an imaginary realm projected not by the pictures but by the text. While the admittedly banal text falls far short of other fantastic journeys of this type (such as Lewis Carroll's *Alice in Wonderland*, which would appear two decades later, or Jonathan Swift's *Gulliver's Travels*, which had already appeared in 1726), the sixty-three illustrations reveal an expanded pictorial space that, as the frontispiece shows from the start, appears to swallow up the entire world. These proliferating images in the *Voyages où il vous plaira* are travel pictures — even if of a peculiar type — that function also as therapy for the travel mania that had gripped the nineteenth century. The pictures are deployed as a remedy for what afflicts the traveler, driving out his wanderlust through the prescribed readings. Wanderlust is also what the protagonist of the story does not wish to relinquish entirely, as he fears with some justification that his wedding will not lead him to far-off realms but rather leave him at home within the confines of four walls. How can "leaving and remaining," "remaining and leaving," be reconciled with each other? How can one remain at home and still get away? How can one remain true to the old life and yet still seize hold of the new one? For surely the wedding cannot be the last journey taken . . . And so the answer is, no more travel, but instead read, and travel nonetheless.

On the night before his wedding, Franz battles his emerging wanderlust and first invokes de Maistre: "'Why does the wise de Maistre's type of travel no longer satisfy me!' I called aloud. 'Why can't I, like him, satisfy my passion, such that I am able to travel through the world without leaving my room! Oh, the burning desire within me to see everything, will it never cease?'" (Johannot 15). And when that does not work, either, and the wanderlust begins to stir again, Franz burns the alluring and accursed *Histoire*

VOYAGE OÙ IL VOUS PLAIRA

08.0 Frontispiece to Tony Johannot, Alfred de Musset, and P.-J. Stahl, *Voyage où il vous plaira* (Paris, 1979).

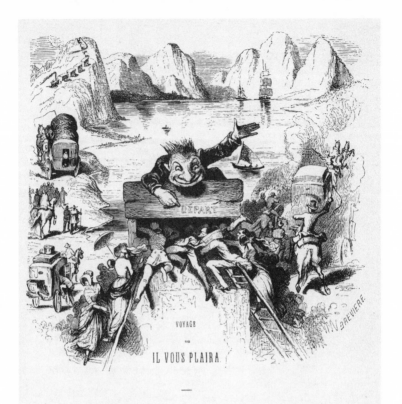

VOYAGE

OU

IL VOUS PLAIRA.

—

AVANT-PROPOS

Il serait peut-être bon, cher lecteur, et, à coup sûr, il serait convenable de vous dire pourquoi nous partons, où nous allons, et aussi quelles raisons nous pouvons avoir pour désirer qu'il vous plaise de venir avec nous?

08.1 Preface; in Tony Johannot, Alfred de Musset, and P.-J. Stahl, *Voyage où il vous plaira* (Paris, 1979), 1.

générale des voyages (Johannot 21). Yet when he throws the last chunk of book into the fire, it begins to crackle like ice on a windowpane that takes on a thousand bizarre forms and landscapes, such that the text turns into images. The burning book becomes an imaginary travel album that permeates memory with visions, and indeed memory and reading themselves turn into visions. The reader can experience these visions in the form of the stories and images, and share the fever of Franz's travel dream. For at midnight — when else? — he falls asleep until someone knocks and his friend Jean Walter appears, who not only shares his wanderlust but also is the one who first turned him on to travel. However, Jean Walter appears to have turned into a ghost and, as the images and text indicate, into a diabolical creature that once again seduces Franz into traveling, as well as into first passing by the room of his fiancée. There follows a journey that lasts throughout the night, dream sequence following upon dream sequence that often makes use of the stylistic device of the dream within a dream. The web of images becomes ever more dense, turning into a nightmare from which not even the murder of his companion, who wants to abscond with Franz's bride, releases him, since this only transforms Jean Walter into two beings that haunt him from then on as the living and the dead, as Jean and as Walter. The two meet a man without a brain, talk with flower girls, meet a man weary of life, whom they advise to travel as a distraction, and even meet the allegorical Hope. It's a journey without aim whose destination provides an excuse "for those who have nothing to do" (Johannot 86), and the traveler himself has "no rationale, only the love of movement in and of itself in order to constantly roam from place to place" (ibid.). At the same time, the traveler sits motionless in his armchair, even though his life takes a different direction as a result of this journey. Despite all this error and confusion, the journey has a clear meaning, which appears indeed when Franz awakens and appreciates his wedding as the chance for a new life, one that will

Franz ne s'aperçut qu'il était couvert de neige qu'en se retrouvant
au coin de son feu.

08.2 Franz; in Tony Johannot, Alfred de Musset, and P.-J. Stahl, *Voyage où il vous plaira* (Paris, 1979), 10.

Brulez, brulez, m'écriai-je, vous qui m'avez perdu....

... Je retombai sans force dans mon fauteuil.

08.3 Brulez; in Tony Johannot, Alfred de Musset, and P.-J. Stahl, *Voyage où il vous plaira* (Paris, 1979), 20.

have nothing to do with travel, though at least reading will serve as a means of travel through a new type of book. It is a dramatic story of salvation, death, downfall, friendship, and finally the bourgeois existence as last resort. Amid hopeless circumstances, as the ship threatens to go down amid the sea of images, once again there comes a knock at the door. It is his servant, who does not bring him his traveling clothes, but rather his wedding suit — and thus a new life free of travel begins. The restlessness that mutated into a dream of cluelessness is now at an end. Franz awakens "next to my pipe, whose smoke is mixed with confused memories from my years of travel which all the spirits of this restless night had awakened" (Johannot 161) as he swears off travel for good. Though in lieu of travel, which the text repeatedly presents more as a therapy for melancholy, there remains the reading of illustrated books to help fight off, when necessary, the onset of dejection. The journey through the sea of images transforms the traveling life into a life of reading, and life into a dream that makes *Voyages où vous plaira* possible anytime. All you need do is to pick up a book and let yourself be carried away on the sea of images.

Travel Reading

Forster, Léon. *Voyages au coin du feu.* Third edition. Tours, 1850.

Goethe, Johann Wolfgang. *Die Leiden des jungen Werthers: Die Wahlverwandtschaften; Kleine Prosa. Epen.* Ed. Waltraud Wiethölter with Christoph Brecht. Frankfurt am Main, 2006.

Hetzel, Pierre-Jules. *Un éditeur et son siècle.* Saint-Sébastien, 1988.

Johannot, Tony, Alfred de Musset, and P.-J. Stahl. *Voyage où il vous plaira.* Paris, 1979 (facsimile of first edition, Paris, 1843).

Schilling, August. *Vogelperspektiven eines Wanderlustigen.* Vienna, 1847.

Dark Chambers

Tell me, how is it that images from a dark chamber reproduce
nature with astounding fidelity; I have no other word by which
to describe the beauty of this fleeting impression; everything
is there: expression, precise forms, color; it is nature and yet
more than nature, the blown up or reduced facial features
being particularly easier to appreciate. I could continually look
at the face of my lady friend, which looks so alive.

De Maistre, 101

Xavier de Maistre, the first room traveler, was also one of the first
to witness a discovery that in the nineteenth century introduced
a lasting visual revolution, and also had consequences for travel
in general: photography. De Maistre writes as an eyewitness to
the daguerreotypes of his friend Rodolphe Toepffer, whose *Voyages en zigzag* became not only — along with *Voyage autour de ma
chambre* — one of the most frequently quoted texts of later room
journeys but also one of the most important early engagements
with the new technical medium that de Maistre ironically and re-
spectfully referred to in his letters as "métaphysique du daguer-
rotipe (sic!)" ("metaphysics of the daguerreotype") (de Maistre
105). De Maistre provides new material for consideration in the
form of reports of his personal observations. Unusually early for
a Frenchman, in a letter from October 29, 1841, he concerns himself with William Henry Fox Talbot's method and the discovery by

Joseph Berres, whom he knew personally (de Maistre 100–102). And about Louis Daguerre's photos he already writes on February 28, 1839, in an extensive postscript to a letter: "You have no doubt read about the invention of Mr. Daguerre in the papers," he writes to Toepffer. "He has found the means by which to fix images developed through the camera obscura. I have already seen these marvelous images and believe that you will be pleased to have the account of an eyewitness to whom the inventor has announced what he thinks of his own invention" (de Maistre 19).

The room traveler is understandably fascinated by photography and these images from the camera obscura, and he describes in detail the technical process, but also the aesthetic effects.* For him photography is, like for many of his generation, a natural wonder, a result of the power of nature, a simulacrum of reality. It is, according to de Maistre, the sun that does the work—and with amazing precision: "The presentation misses nothing: objects which one can hardly see in the distance with one's own eyes are reproduced with exceptional exactitude; the picture of a telegraph operator, who in the dark chamber is reduced to a hardly perceptible size can be observed so precisely with a magnifying glass that one can almost see the message being conveyed" (de Maistre 20). The same goes for a shot of Daguerre's studio, in which a statue can be observed with the highest possible clarity. And thus his verdict—in contrast to Toepffer's—is exceedingly positive: even if the sky is sometimes a bit dark, architectural shots or those of statues or interiors are like "nature itself" (de Maistre 21).

When what is captured in the dark chamber of the camera obscura consists not only of images but also of the objects them-

---

* In regard to photography, see also Alfred Berthier, *Xavier de Maistre: Etude biographique et littéraire*, 1918, p. 167 f., as well as Xavier de Maistre, *Lettres à sa famille*, ed. Gabriel de Maistre, 3 vols. (Clermond-Ferrand) 2005 (vol. 1) and 2006 (vols. 2 and 3), especially in vol. 1 the entry on daguerreotypes on p. 204, as well as Toepffer's book on daguerreotypes, p. 236.

09.0 Hoer, *Room Journey*; in Stephan Oettermann, ed., *Sehnsucht: Das Panorama als Massenunterhaltung des 19. Jahrhunderts* (Basel, 1993), 217.

selves that have been turned into images (as the American professor of medicine and publisher Oliver Wendell Holmes observed in several articles on the consequences of the early media theory of the simulacrum, one of which also appeared in book form in *Soundings from the Atlantic* in 1859), journeys of exploration are no longer necessary — an estimation shared by Peter Altenberg a half century later based on the existence of the postcard and his nearly manic collecting of them (Altenberg 269): photography makes travel simply superfluous, for indeed, as Holmes notes further, one could even do away with buildings once they materialize in photos. And one can almost physically wander around photos: "I creep over the vast features of Rameses, on the face of his rock-hewn Nubian temple; I scale the huge mountain-crystal that calls itself the Pyramid of Cheops. I pace the length of the three titanic stones in the wall of Baalbec — mightiest masses of quarried rock that man has lifted into the air. . . . I look into the eyes of the caged tiger, and on the scaly train of the crocodile, stretched on the sands of the river that has mirrored a hundred dynasties. I stroll through Rheinish vineyards, I sit under Roman arcades, I walk the streets of once buried cities, I look into the chasms of Alpine glaciers, and on the rush of wasteful cataracts" (Holmes 153–54).

Yet before the discovery of photography there were technical advances in media designed to use images to replace travel. Therefore it's no wonder that many of these optical apparatuses are used explicitly to describe room travel. At the start of the nineteenth century, cosmoramas, "perspective-optical room journeys," as they were called at the time, came into style (Oettermann 47). In the room journey of Lexa and Wild, some of "those interested in travel or seeing sights . . . could behold at their leisure some of the most beautiful cities and landscapes without hardly taking a step and at very little cost, and if the onlooker employs just a bit of fantasy, thus through these well-done copies of nature he will be able to pass his time with as much pleasure as if he were to stand in front of the original settings themselves" (Oettermann 48, quoting the *Theaterzeitung*, Vienna, December 8, 1823, p. 588).[†] Of-

---

[†] Advertised on the placard: "An exceptionally large display of a magical, functional, and graphic room journey." C. Hoer, Vienna, 1924. "Voyage en chambre magique."

09.1 Underwood and Underwood, stereophoto; in Maureen C. O'Brien and Mary Bergstein, eds., *Image and Enterprise: The Photographs of Adolphe Braun* (London, 2000), 99.

fered was the "Ascent of Mont Blanc," the "Route of the Overland Mail to India," or "Hamilton's Delightful Excursion to the Continent and Back within Two Hours." And occasionally next to the entrance there would also be a display of travel literature for people to use, or one could pick up small brochures in which the show was further expanded on. The Hamburg critic Moritz G. Saphir wrote about Karl Georg Enslen's 1827 exhibition of room journeys in Berlin: "To sit in a room and still be able to travel is much more comfortable than having to deal with the dust or customs control or visas that inconvenience the traveler" (von Plessen 207).

In 1828, Enslen also had his *Führer auf Enslen's malerischer Reise* (*Guide to Enslen's Pictorial Journeys*) printed in order to promote "the panoramic paintings gathered on my travels to towns and sites, some of them painted later on, others painted directly on the spot" (Enslen iii). The viewer could see new images of Pompei and the "Grand Duchal Plaza in Florence." Both are, or so the prospectus announces in full-throated manner, "near to perfection" (Enslen iv). Especially Pompei is one of the most beloved motifs for panoramas, cosmoramas, and dioramas — and incidentally also for later photography that used it to attract sales — since in addition to a view of an archaeological site it made possible a type of time travel, and allowed the observer to step into Roman antiquity. For Enslen, "viewing an old, lovely way of life from a world and time that has also just newly appeared, and which allows one to observe vividly the smallest of things, is of inexpressible interest to the sophisticated traveler among the rubble" (Enslen 43). Viewing and wandering, rubble and resurrection, go hand in hand here. The journey made from home through the camera obscura provides such links. In 1933, and thus more than a century later, Walter Benjamin dedicated one of his writings to these panoramas which appeared in the *Frankfurter Zeitung*, and then also in the autobiographical notes to *Berliner Kindheit um neunzehnhundert* (*Berlin Childhood around 1900*), where it was reprinted as "Kaiser-panorama." Benjamin describes there his visit to this "aquarium of the distant and the past" (Benjamin 325), whose magic even in the year 1900 belonged to the past, but which still fascinated children. Picture after picture presented shots of far-off places to the viewer, who indeed amid all these picture journeys reflected on his homey room from within and while crossing such a distance: "Because this is what was special about such journeys: that their distant worlds were never strange and that the desire that they awoke within me was not always the allure of the unknown, but rather much more frequently alleviated the desire to return home" (Benjamin 326).

And already by the mid-nineteenth century, there really was no need to leave one's room to commence such visual journeys, for one could do so through stereoscopes or photo collections. With the help of photography (which resulted from different journeys conceived for just such purposes), journeys of exploration became possible at home, such as that of Louis de Cormenin, which he made in 1852 through Maxine Du Camp's photographs of the Orient, which Du Camp took on a trip with Gustave Flaubert: "We no longer need to board Cook's or Lapeyrousse's ship in order to risk journeying at breakneck speed; heliography, which is left to certain daredevils, takes us around the world and brings the universe to us in a wallet without our having to leave our chair" (de Cormenin 124 f.). And one no longer needed to tap the power of the imagination to produce images that lived up to how far-off places were imagined to be, for the viewers now ascribed to photography a reality that could not be doubted. The images logged by the camera obscura of the camera's apparatus were a manifest near distance that could be wandered through with one's eyes — always in search of new details and discoveries. When in 1859 photography was first allowed into the Paris Salon, even if it was in a separate building, an important step was taken, as Benjamin mentions in the notes to *The Arcades Project*, by presenting, "at the Salon de Photographie in 1859, numerous 'voyages' to Egypt, to Jerusalem, to Greece, to Spain. In his account, Figuier observes: 'Hardly had the practical processes of photography on paper come to be understood than a whole band of operators rushed forth . . . in all directions, to bring us back views of monuments, buildings, and ruins taken in all known lands of the world.' Hence the new *voyages photographiques*" (Benjamin, *Arcades*, 684–85).

09.2 Advertisement for Johann Michael Sattler's *Panorama of Salzburg and Optical Room Journey*, 1830; in Ursula Storch, *Zauber der Ferne: Imaginäre Reisen im 19. Jahrhundert* (Vienna, 2009), 88.

And thanks to the stereoscope, since the middle of the century even three-dimensional views could be photographically produced. In the 1850s, the stereoscope was one of the first optical forms of mass media in any bourgeois household. Millions of different motifs, which were purchased singularly or in series, were available. Nearly every stretch of land could be seen in pictures, and nearly every far-off journey could now be tackled right at home with the stereoscope before one's eyes. An Augsburg brochure from 1858 advertised the stereoscope also as a new form of room travel: "With this simple (stereo) apparatus you can commence your wanderings right in your room and spend some time on a Swiss glacier or a wildly romantic mountain range, or soon find yourself on the lovely banks of the Rhine and the Elba or turn your gaze to architecture's wonderful creations" ("Das Stereoskop und die Lichtbilder" 150).

And in opposite manner, photography also had the effect that journeys were made into the near-at-hand and documented through photos. With the photographer Ildéfonse Rousset, the French writer Émile Gigaule de la Bédollière visited the Boise de Vicennes, which like today is a few minutes from the center of Paris, and thereby accomplished a *tour de Marne*. Both journeys were documented through original photographs in lavish publications that were completely different from one copy to another, and that also supplied postcards and extensive information on the areas visited near Paris. Such photographic expeditions made to local sites were not at all rare. Numerous photo albums survive that are not devoted to distant lands, but rather document the nearby distances of the near-at-hand—an approach that still is used today. Bernard Hermann, to name just one example, perhaps was fortunate enough to live right near the Cathedral of Notre Dame in Paris. He lived in an apartment on the corner of the rue de Seine and the rue de Saint-Jacques. For six years, he photographed only what went on outside his windows, and then brought together in one volume a selection from this enormous fund of pictures. He selected a total of 96 photographs, which were then broken down into categories in the table of contents: 36 of them were taken with a 500mm zoom lens, 12 with 1000mm zoom, 69 in horizontal format and 27 vertical; 26 of the 96 photographs were of Notre Dame, 5 of flying pigeons, and 2 of them self-portraits of the photographer while photographing. When he was asked if it bothered him to stay in one place the whole time, he answered "that the Earth's rotation allowed him to travel 30,000 kilometers a day without the least bother, and thus he saw no need to add any more pitter-patter" (Hermann, no page). Since Notre Dame is the starting point for measuring any distance, he titled his book *Paris, km 00*, to supply this symbolically laden ground zero with even more meaning: "An entryway into the universe through a very narrow prism. Kilometer zero is like an aleph: the entire world comes together there" (Hermann, no page).

Many thousands of kilometers away, we find another form of photographic travel: Heike Behrend writes about a peculiar practice in the photo studios of Mombasa, Kenya. The pictures don't show what is there, such as the ferry to Zanzibar, but rather what is not there, such as the attractions of Nairobi, which then later lead us to surmise that we have been in Nairobi. The photo studio has a number of such views ready as mountable backgrounds, from which someone not wishing to travel to such places can choose. And then if doubts should be raised later on, we can then turn to the surety of the photographic evidence, because if a picture shows something from far off, the camera must have also gone along for the journey. In Heidelberg, it is a long-established practice to relieve the travel-weary Japanese from having to climb up to the castle: the bus driver simply collects all their cameras in order to take the same picture from the same perspective with each one while the tourists go shopping or take a break.

Travel Reading

Altenberg, Peter. *Mein Lebensabend*. Berlin, 1919.
Bédollière, Émile Gigaule de la. *Le Bois de Vincennes*. Paris, 1867.

————. *Le tour de Marne*. Paris, 1865.

Behrend, Heike. "Imaginäre Reise: Die Likoni-Ferry-Fotografen in Mombasa/Kenia." *Fotogeschichte*. Vol. 19, no. 71, 1999. 25–34.

Benjamin, Walter. *The Arcades Project*. Trans. Howard Eiland and Kevin McLaughlin. Cambridge, 1999.

————. "Kaiserpanorama." In Benjamin, *Medienästhetische Schriften*. Frankfurt am Main, 2002. 325f.

Cormenin, Louis de. "A propos de l'Égypte, Nubie, Palestine, et Syrie, de Maxime Du Camp (1852)." In *André Rouillé: La photographie en France*. Paris, 1859. 124f.

Enslen, Karl Georg. *Führer auf Enslen's malerischer Reise im Zimmer*. Berlin, 1828.

Gläser, Franz (Joseph), composer. *Menagerie und optische Zimmerreise in Krähwinkel* (first performed February 22, 1825, in Vienna).

Hermann, Bernard. *Paris, km 00: Photographies d'un voyage en chambre*. Paris, 2006.

Holmes, Oliver Wendell. "The Stereoscope and the Stereograph." In *Soundings from the Atlantic*. Boston, 1864. 124–65.

Maistre, Xavier de. *Lettres à sa famille*. Ed. Gabriel de Maistre. 3 vols. Clermond-Ferrand, 2005 (vol. 1) and 2006 (vols. 2 and 3).

————. *Lettres inédites à son ami Töpffer*. Ed. Léon-A. Matthey. Geneva, 1945.

Oettermann, Stephan. "Die Reise mit den Augen—'Oramas' in Deutschland." In Marie-Louise von Plessen, *Sehnsucht: Das Panorama als Massenunterhaltung des 19. Jahrhunderts*. Basel, 1993. 42–51.

Plessen, Marie-Louise von. *Sehnsucht: Das Panorama als Massenunterhaltung des 19. Jahrhunderts*. Basel, 1993.

Starl, Timm. *Kritik der Fotografie*. http://www.kritik-der-fotografie.at/28-Reisen.htm.

"Das Stereoskop und die Lichtbilder als die schönsten Eroberungen des fortschreitenden Erfindergeistes," Verlag G. Geiger,

Augsburg, 1858. In Ursula Peters, *Stilgeschichte der Fotografie in Deutschland, 1839–1900*. Köln, 1979. 150.

Toepffer, Rodolphe. *De la place Daguerre: À propos des excursions daguerriennes* (1841). Cognac, 2002. (First published, Paris, 1852.)

Interiors

One does not start out on a journey around the world in the same way that one starts out for a stroll.

Kierkegaard, 163

The nineteenth century, like no other century, was addicted to dwelling. It conceived the residence as a receptacle for the person, and it encased him with all his appurtenances so deeply in the dwelling's interior that one might be reminded of the inside of a compass case, where the instrument with all its accessories lies embedded in deep, usually violet folds of velvet.

Benjamin, 220

The peculiar transformation of an apartment into a microcosm that contains an entire world can be found in almost every description of an interior in nineteenth-century literature. Objects are turned into symbols of their owner, who expresses his existence through each one of them, while also seeking to transform them into miniatures of the external world. The interior is an inner realm that materializes in objects and takes shape from the apartment itself. Leberecht Hühnchen, who in his time was *the* literary incarnation of the Biedermeier man, and who with the writer Heinrich Seidel attained huge success at the end of the nineteenth century, thus describes his residence as a "microcosm" in which we can "delight in all temperature zones and climates." And once the home is widely thought of in such manner, the idea of a journey around the world within our own four walls is no longer difficult to imagine. "Let us begin our wandering, here at the north end," he writes, extending an invitation for a trip around the world to the reader so inclined. "Right next to the window we find the frigid zone and can reach out to touch the polar ice. Next we move south and already manage to find ourselves in the moderate zone here in this rocking chair. A tropical breeze blows upon us from the furnace at the end of the wide hall. This furnace represents the Tropic of Cancer. We pass it and find ourselves in the midst of the hot zone. The sofa, which invites us to lie down and rest, is Cameroon. . . . What you take to be cracks in the wooden floor are the lines of latitude, and this one here, somewhat deeper than the rest, marks the equator. Accordingly, we find ourselves already in the Southern Hemisphere, and by stepping through this open door into the second room, we find there again a furnace, which is the Tropic of Capricorn. Slowly we walk through the southern temperate and frigid zones until we again encounter polar ice. And look, all of this in the space of a few seconds, nor do we need seven-mile-high boots like Peter Schlemihl, who, while he was botanizing in the North found a polar bear standing in his path, and in his bewilderment he staggered through all climates, first cold, then hot, whereby he came down with a massive lung infection. We can do the same much more comfortably in just our slippers. And now for some coffee!" (Seidel 25 f.). And this one awaited eagerly, since the polar ice, even when there was hardly any fear of freezing, was so close by.

Leberecht Hühnchen is Peter Schlemihl as room traveler, one who in pajamas paces off his apartment and in the process transforms all its components into geographic coordinates. His astronomical tropics are light-years away from those of Henry Miller a half century later. Here a space is depicted that freely and irrationally takes in the world and arranges it according to house rules,

10.0 Sasha Stone, *Bourgeois Interior*; in *Walter Benjamin Archive: Bilder, Texte und Zeichen* (Frankfurt am Main, 2006), 225.

which then become for the occupant life rules. The space is sealed off from the outside and acknowledges no reality beyond its own four walls: it is self-sufficient.

In the literature of the nineteenth century there are many descriptions of this type, and paintings of interiors also seek in many ways to display the visible room with all its objects and configurations, such that the viewer can also perceive the inhabitant's presence in the things depicted, even if he is not visible in the picture itself. Living space is not just the space of the inhabitant—it is his world. "Interiors," so Karl Schlögel reflects, "are worlds in miniature, universes, living spaces, vessels of the private man, the private woman. Interiors as such are artificial worlds. Within them we can travel the world or journey to the past without ever leaving the room, the ideal place for the 'search for lost time.' We realize what holds the world together only when this inner space is endangered and can be abandoned" (Schlögel 328).

In Søren Kierkegaard's early unfinished philosophical tale "Johannes Climacus," written in 1842–43, there is a room journey that also tries to understand the theoretical underpinnings of the interior, yet introduces a note of doubt about the room and the self. The room is equated with the self, and the interior becomes the space of that self. It then follows that to the passionate walker and travel-shy "street philosopher"* Kierkegaard, such a space provides him with refuge from the trials and tribulations of his experience, which at a minimum have to do with the complex history of his engagement to Regine Olsen and its dissolution. Yet the room is much more than a space where such troubles are not only spelled out and set forth but also lived and written down, indeed where the story of them originates. The room becomes a place of doubt, a place of thought, and an expression of existence as such. And Kierkegaard's enhanced autobiographical depiction of a room journey that Johannes Climacus undertakes with his father, and that, according to his biographer Joakim Garff, "becomes a *must* in any biography" (Garff 36), serves as a fictional-biographical foundation for the philosophical profile of his literary figure, whose love is entirely for the life of the mind and thought. Whoever knows what it means to travel through his childhood within his

---

*Joakim Garff dedicates a chapter of his biography (365–74) to the "Straßenphiloso-phen" ("philosopher of the streets") Kierkegaard.

10.1 Mihály Munkácsy, *Paris Interior*, 1877; in Sabine Schulze, ed., *Innenleben: Die Kunst des Intérieurs; Vermeer bis Kabakov* (Ostfildern-Ruit, 1998), 221.

house also understands, so the argument follows, why his mind can become a "self-contained space" that no longer needs anything from the outside: "His home," so Kierkegaard writes, "did not offer many diversions, and, since he practically never went out, he very early became accustomed to being occupied with himself and with his own thoughts. . . . When at times Johannes asked permission to go out, his request was usually refused; but occasionally his father, by way of compensation, offered to take his hand and go for a walk up and down the floor. At first glance, this was a poor substitute, and yet, like the rough homespun coat, it concealed something altogether different. The offer was accepted, and it was left entirely up to Johannes to decide where they should go for a walk. They walked through the city gate to the country palace nearby or to the seashore or about the streets — according to Johannes's wish, for his father was capable of everything. While they walked up and down the floor, his father would tell about everything they saw. They greeted the passers-by; the carriages rumbled past, drown-

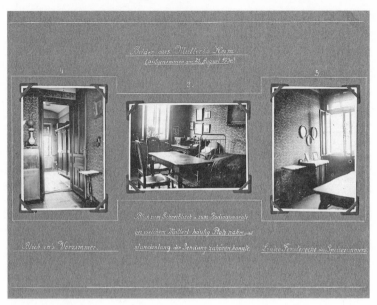

10.2 Mother's house, 1930; author's collection.

ing out his father's voice; the pastry woman's fruits were more tempting than ever" (Kierkegaard 119–20).

The magical skill of the power of the imagination transforms the room into a city full of pleasures at the ready—and all this without setting foot outside the door. The dialogic form is therefore very important, though it is soon "drowned out" by the imagined, intensive, and synesthetic impressions of the room journey that then echo within the self. Thus just as Johannes Climacus as a child transforms with his father the grains of the floorboards into a world that is turned step by step into stories, so the twenty-one-year-old philosophy student would later transform the world into a line of thought that we can climb step by step like a ladder. Kierkegaard's choice of the pseudonym Johannes Climacus, which harkens back to a bishop of the Sinai cloister who wrote the "Paradise Letter" that lays out the soul's path to heaven in thirty steps, is used as part of an imaginary journey through the mind by which

the nature of human existence is laid out. The adventure of the dialectic awaits he who hunkers down inside his room like Robinson
Crusoe on his island, who also is mentioned in the text and whose
sea journey provides the philosopher with an extended metaphor
for his room journey (Kierkegaard 147, 159). "This again was an
adventure that inspired him. In this way his life was always adven-
turous. He did not require forests and travels for his adventures
but merely what he had: a little room with one window" (Kierkegaard 124). The greatest adventure is therefore that of doubt,
which marks not only the beginning of philosophy in general and
the new philosophy in particular, but also an existential problem,
"the solution to which his life depends on" (Pieper 41). While for
Johannes Climacus on the journey with his father the world leads
to the conception of the self, for students of philosophy such reflections turn into an appreciation of the world through the terms
and principle of *ego cogito*: the world becomes the self, the self the
world. The philosophy of German idealism — which Kierkegaard
at a minimum encountered with high interest through Friedrich
von Schelling's lectures in Berlin, abandoning the latter, after
his initial enthusiasm, while remarking, "Schelling's preaching
is unbearable" (Garff 251) — left its traces behind, but at the same
time is reformulated. Doubt, which comes to the forefront through
Kierkegaard and turns the room journey into a philosophical journey of the mind, now intercedes as *interest*, as "*Zwischen-Sein*."
Thus Søren Kierkegaard, alias Johannes Climacus, defines consciousness as a relation, as a gap between the reflections of the
self and reality, which then carries forward into the manifestation
of existence. The room journey is thus transformed into a journey through all of existence that encapsulates both the self and the
world, and delineates the *stages of life's journey*, as the outlines of
existence.

In his notes to *The Arcades Project*, Walter Benjamin quotes (as,
incidentally, does Theodor W. Adorno in his book on the Danish

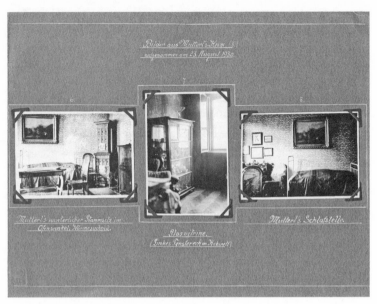

10.3 Mother's house, 1930; author's collection.

philosopher) Kierkegaard's room journey from Eduard Geismar's 1929 book in order to immediately comment, "So the *flâneur* goes for a walk in his room" (Benjamin 421). For Benjamin, Kierkegaard is the emblematic incarnation of that nineteenth-century figure, namely the *flâneur*, for whom the near and the far are dialectic figures, and who is most at home in the *arcade*, that place that is at once both a building and a street. And Kierkegaard also shows up in other parts of *The Arcades Project* — in the shape of a quote from *Stages of Life's Journey*: "'The art would be to be able to feel homesick, even though one is at home.' This," according to Benjamin, "is the formula for the interior" (Benjamin 218). Near and far, present and past, inner and outer space, subject and object, coalesce within the interior, just as on the journey through it — an indissoluble constellation that for Benjamin becomes a key to the nineteenth century, and whose decipherment he undertakes. The interior, "for the private man, represents the universe. In the interior, he brings together the far away and the long ago. His living room is a box in the theater of the world" (Benjamin 9).

Travel Reading

Benjamin, Walter. *The Arcades Project*. Trans. Howard Eiland and Kevin McLaughlin. Cambridge, 1999.

Garff, Joakim. *Sören Kierkegaard: Biographie*. Munich/Vienna, 2004.

Kierkegaard, Søren. "Johannes Climacus." In *Kierkegaard's Writings*, vol. 7. Trans. Howard N. and Edna H. Hong. Princeton, 1985. 113–72.

Pieper, Annemarie. *Søren Kierkegaard*. Munich, 2000. 38–47.

Schlögel, Karl. *Im Raume lesen wir die Zeit: Über Zivilisationsgeschichte und Geopolitik*. Frankfurt am Main, 2006.

Schultze, Sabine, ed. *Innenleben: Die Kunst des Intérieurs; Vermeer bis Kabakov*. Ostfildern-Ruit, 1998.

Seidel, Heinrich. "Die Reise zum Südpol." In Leberecht Hühnchen, *Prosa-Idyllen*. Frankfurt am Main, 1985. 75–78.

The *Flâneur*

Every large city is a little world.

  Fournel, *London and Paris* (1802), quoted in Brüggemann, 11

The least explored land today is Paris itself.

  Houssaye, 148

Thus a person is a mobile and ardent daguerreotype that
records the smallest of impressions and through the flux of
passing things, the bustling life of the city, the multifaceted
physiognomy of public opinion, reproduces the views, the
dislikes, and the biases of the crowd.

  Fournel, 309

When according to Victor Fournel the *flâneur* sets off on his passage through the city, before he leaves he invokes the muses. As the
title "Die Odyssee eines Flaneurs in den Straßen von Paris" makes
clear, Fournel definitely sees himself in the tradition of Odysseus,
though the muses have long since given way to someone new.
"Muse of Flânerie, dreamy virgin with swaying arms, with flow-
ing hair, with loosened girdle, lovable and lighthearted companion
of Sterne and Toepffer, of Hoffmann and Xavier de Maistre, you
are the one whom I invoke today!" (Fournel 308). Once the Muse
of Flânerie is invoked and is named a literary classic, the path is

almost laid. It's already been trod, according to Fournel, by Laurence Sterne in his *Sentimental Journey*, by Rodolphe Toepffer with his *Voyages en zigzag*, by E. T. A. Hoffmann with his view through "My Cousin's Corner Window," and not least of all by Xavier de Maistre, thanks especially to his *Voyage autour de ma chambre*. Yet differently from these wanders the Odysseus of the nineteenth century through a city — and not just any city, but indeed Paris, a city that in the imagination of its literati is turned into a world unto itself, into primeval forest, into a new America in which, as in Alexandre Dumas' *Les Mohicans de Paris*, bands of Indians (which in reality appear from the city's underworld) stir up trouble; and into a single remaining Orient, more precisely a fusion of Orient and Occident, of culture and nature, of moving and eventful stories and their ability to capture the reader. The dream world of the Orient, of the East, of the rising sun, occurs now in a city in which, with the arrival of artificial light, the sun never sets, and which therefore never sleeps: "The Orient is nowhere else but in Paris. Only in Paris are there primeval forests. There is nothing new under the sun, meaning under the sun of Paris" (Houssaye 149). In the nineteenth century, Paris is the city that invented the *flâneur* and celebrated him as the one who discovers the cityscape as an urbane cosmos. This becomes a space that can be inhabited just like a room. "Parisians make the street an interior," states Walter Benjamin, before concluding: "The intoxicated interpenetration of street and residence . . . has prophetic value" (Benjamin, *Arcades*, 421 and 423). For Benjamin, the transformation of the cityscape constitutes the experience of the *flâneur*, yet under his gaze it exists in dialectical fashion and marks a new kind of spatial experience: "It becomes a landscape that opens up to him and a parlor that encloses him" (Benjamin, "Return of the *Flâneur*," 263).

Some decades later, at the beginning of the twentieth century, Berlin tried to emulate Paris by depicting itself as a world-class city in this sense. "Each square meter of Berlin contains the entire world," alleged Leonhard Frank (Frank 2). Here as in Paris, the city is seen as a microcosm, only a small part of which one needs to wander through while exploring it with the *flâneur*'s roaming gaze. In Paris as well as later in Berlin, one can, so long as one has eyes to see, discover a New World much like Columbus. "Christopher Columbus discovered America more or less as a *flâneur* upon the ocean. There remain many new Americas to discover when one enters certain unexplored neighborhoods of the Parisian ocean on his own as a *flâneur*" (Fournel 310). And similarly, Franz Hessel, the Berlin *flâneur* par excellence, states half a century later, with recourse to the French language: "So everything becomes more multiple, new things appear both near and far, and the wonderful mixture of each, *où l'indécis au précis se joint* (where the undefined and the precise meet)" (Hessel, *Flaneur*, 145).

Journeys of discovery within the near-at-hand—that is *flânerie*. Yet it's much less about the discovery of new worlds than it is about something newly discovered about supposedly old, familiar ones, which—as with de Maistre's room traveler—is first tapped by the gaze of the traveling *flâneur*. So writes Louis Sébastien Mercier in the foreword to *Tableaux de Paris*: "Many inhabitants of Paris are strangers to their own city: perhaps this book will have something to offer them, or at least cast the life and goings-on that surround them, which because of long habit they no longer even perceive, into new, sharper light before their very eyes" (*Mein Bild von Paris* [*My Picture of Paris*], quoted in Köhn 7). While Mercier describes here a way of becoming familiar with surroundings that have become strange, later texts define it as a process of active estrangement, as a calculated retreat from the recognizable, the familiar, the homey. Whether in the room or in the city, the spirit with which the journey is carried out transforms the near into a distant unknown, into a wonderland. The *flâneur* is a traveler in the near-at-hand. So Benjamin notes in his *The Arcades Project*, that theoretical-philosophical travel guide for the *flâneur*: "The

11.0 Queens Arcade, Leeds, 1889; in Johann Friedrich Geist, *Passagen ein Bautyp des 19. Jahrhunderts* (Munich, 1969), no. 94.

flâneur puts on the costume of the voyager in Maxime Du Camp's 'Le voyageur': 'I am afraid to stop — it's the engine of my life'" (Benjamin, *Arcades*, 430). And thus Victor Fournel asks what lies buried behind the concept of the *flâneur* in order to link the activities of *flânerie* with those of a journey, to such a degree as to provide

11.1 Germaine Krull, *Passage du Caire in Paris*; in *Walter Benjamin Archive: Bilder, Texte und Zeichen* (Frankfurt am Main, 2006), 215.

an itinerary for his travels: "to undertake continual research trips through the streets and on the promenades" (Fournel 310). Hence a *flâneur* makes discoveries just like a researcher does. For Fournel, the exploration of the cityscape in the spirit of the journey taken with sharpened eyes is a program comparable to that of the biologist on the one hand, and the novelist on the other. "Nothing escapes my gaze, which is able to look through the most impenetrable darkness; at least I think so, and that's all I need. Each individual detail provides me with something, if somehow I want to develop such material into a novel. And so, like Cuvier, who reconstructs an entire animal from a tooth, and from a single animal an entire world, I reconstruct life that has been broken into pieces and turned into dust. I call this the Theater of the Automatons, whose threads I hold in my hand to pull, ponder, and manipulate just as I please" (Fournel 309). Thus the *flâneur* is the promenading god of the city who realizes his full potential only by observing.

Just as for the room traveler Xavier de Maistre the old, familiar space of his room is transformed through his journey, so the usual paths through the city are transformed all at once and alter the view of one's surroundings and oneself. Hessel expressed this in a wonderfully apt observation: "The incomparable appeal of a walk is that it releases us from our more or less exasperating private life. We travel among, and commune with, very strange surroundings and fates. This the genuine walker notes in the strange shock he senses when amid the dream city of his *flânerie* he suddenly meets someone he knows, and after being taken aback, recognizes him as Herr So-and-So on his way home from the office" (Hessel, "Vor der schwierigen Kunst," 57). One loses oneself within and to perceivable things, and from that comes the everyday perception of the self lost amid the tried-and-tested habitation. And by comparison, through *flânerie*, we can develop a new sense of habitation, a new mien that for the very first time makes the city space a living space. And this can then be read like a text. The cultural technique of *flânerie* turns the city, at the historical threshold of its disappearance, into an open book in which we can certainly read much more about the development of its space and the role of the individual within it than about its history. Hessel's decidedly modern *flâneur* knows about the transient nature of his actions and wanders a last time through the spaces that have already begun to radically change. Brecht's dictum "Cover your tracks," from the *Lesebuch für Stadtbewohner* (*A Reader for City Dwellers*), is the motto of a new time that makes the *flâneur* obsolete. "The Tauentzienstraße and the Kurfürstendamm have the important cultural function of teaching Berliners how to be *flâneurs*; otherwise this urbane practice will be lost. But perhaps it's not too late. *Flânerie* is the art of reading the street, whereby people's faces, displayed goods, display windows, café terraces, trams, cars, and trees become prominent and equal letters, which together form the words, sentences, and pages of an ever new book" (Hessel, *Flaneur*, 145).

Walter Benjamin, who worked with Franz Hessel on a translation of Marcel Proust's *In Search of Lost Time*, whose author hardly ever left the space of his room closed off to the outside world, gave Hessel's book *Ein Flaneur in Berlin* a subtle, enthusiastic, and pointed review in which he indeed described the cityscape as a dwelling: "'We Berliners,' says Hessel, 'must inhabit our city much more fully.' He undoubtedly wants this to be understood literally, and to be applied less to the houses than to the streets. For it is they that are the dwelling place of the eternally restless being who is eternally on the move, the being that experiences, learns, knows, and imagines as much between the houses as the individual between the four walls" (Benjamin, "Return of the *Flâneur*," 263–64).

The *flâneur* thus passes through the city as if passing through a room, and brings to this the exact same approach as that which de Maistre saw with different eyes. "Even in Hessel's earlier, masterly 'Vorschule des Journalismus' ('Primer of Journalism')," Benjamin writes, "the question of what 'dwelling' means could be seen as an underlying motif. Just as ever tried-and-true experience also includes its opposite, so here the perfected art of the *flâneur* includes a knowledge of 'dwelling.' The primal image of 'dwelling,' however, is the matrix or shell — that is, the thing which enables us to read off the exact figure of whatever lives inside it" (Benjamin, "Return of the *Flâneur*," 264).

That which here applies to Paris (and Berlin) also speaks to the most prominent place of *flânerie*, which in its time functioned as a city within a city, but which like a Russian nesting doll held the same characteristics as its bigger sister, namely the "arcade." The arcade is constructed, as Benjamin states, "so that [it] is a city, a world in miniature" (Benjamin, *Arcades*, 31). Thus, just as the city functions as both landscape and dwelling for the *flâneur*, so the arcade is both a street and a house. And that is above all also true for Paris, where some of the arcades have survived up to today. Between 1799 and 1830, nineteen arcades were built there, with another seven arriving by 1855 (Köhn 28). Louis Aragon was still exploring them at the beginning of the twentieth century (which was also just at the start of their actual physical disappearance) in his *Pariser Landleben* (*Parisian Country Life*), casting the narrator of his text as a guide who seeks to present before the reader's eyes the discovery of this magical realm of imagination, and the view of it through text and images.

All texts are the same — just as all room journeys are as well, in a certain sense — in that they call on the reader to behave like the narrator and give himself or herself over to the journey. Writes Franz Hessel at the end of his *Ein Flaneur in Berlin*, "Those were a couple of meek attempts to walk around and through Berlin, and now, my dear fellow citizen, don't just rely on what I've said to be important or notable, but walk along by yourself aimlessly as you make your little exploration of the accidental" (Hessel, *Flaneur*, 273). In other places, however, he is more precise: "I'm not here to send you, my fellow aspiring walker, to strange neighborhoods and worthwhile sights. Visit your own city, walk through a neighborhood, wander around the stony garden, step beyond your profession, duties, and habits" (Hessel, "Vor der schwierigen Kunst," 55).

Travel Reading

Aragon, Louis. *Le Paysan de Paris*. Paris, 1926. (German trans., *Pariser Landleben*. Munich, 1969.)

Ardières, O. de l'. *Sur le trottoir: Causéries d'un flâneur*. Paris, 1873.

Benjamin, Walter. *The Arcades Project*. Trans. Howard Eiland and Kevin McLaughlin. Cambridge, 1999.

———. "The Return of the *Flâneur*." In Benjamin, *Selected Writings*, vol. 2. Trans. Rodney Livingstone. Cambridge, 1999. 262–67.

Corajoud, Pierre. *Le Temps d'une flânerie: Impressions d'un aventurier du proche*. Lausanne, 2002.

Fournel, Victor. "Die Odyssee eines Flaneurs in den Straßen von Paris." Excerpt translated into German from *Ce qu'on voit dans les rues de Paris*. Paris, 1858 (here 259–73). In Heinz Brüggemann, *"Aber schickt keinen Poeten nach London!" Großstadt und literarische Wahrnehmung im 18. und 19. Jahrhundert; Texte und Interpretationen*. Reinbek bei Hamburg, 1985. 308–18.

Frank, Leonhard. "Reportage und Dichtung: Eine Rundfrage." *Die Literarische Welt*, no. 26. 1926. 2f.

Gautier, Théophile. "Une promenade au hasard." In Gautier, *Quand on voyage*. Paris, 1865. 337–52.

Hessel, Franz. *Ein Flaneur in Berlin*. Berlin, 1984. (First published as *Spazieren in Berlin*. Vienna, 1929.)

———. "Von der schwierigen Kunst spazieren zu gehen." In *Ermunterung zum Genuß: Kleine Prosa*. Berlin, 1981. 53–61.

Houssaye, Arsène. "Voyage à ma fenêtre." In Houssaye, *Œuvres*, vol. 4. Paris, 1855. 1–225.

Köhn, Eckhardt. *Straßenrausch: Flanerie und kleine Form; Versuch zur Literaturgeschichte des Flaneurs bis 1933*. Berlin, 1989.

Muzard, M. *Voyage d'un flâneur dans les rues de Paris*. Paris, 1839.

Neumeyer, Harald. *Der Flaneur*. Freiburg, 1996.

Noriac, Jules. *Journal d'un flâneur*. Paris, 1865.

EXCURSION AND STOPOVER

Around the World in 80 Days

The surprise and disappointment of traveling. The illusion of
having overcome distance, of having erased time. To be far
away.

Perec, 77

As for looking around the town, he never even gave it a
moment's thought, as he was the sort of Englishman who gets
his servant to do the sights for him.

Verne, 33

Excursion

"All the ships in Jules Verne are perfect cubby-holes, and the vast-
ness of their circumnavigation further increases the bliss of their
closure," observes Roland Barthes in his *Mythologies* (66). Also,
Around the World in 80 Days is, despite the numerous means of
transportation, only an apparent exception. For Verne's Phileas
Fogg, who in 1872 circles the world in eighty days, asks himself at
the end what he actually has left from his trip. It's true that he won
his bet at the Eccentrics Club, but the entire sum that he won was
eaten up by his having to handle the difficulties encountered in ar-
ranging transport — whether it involved purchasing elephants, or
even entire ships, whose wood was later simply burned to achieve

11a.0 Phileas Fogg; in Jules Verne, *Le Tour du monde en quatre-vingts jours* (Lausanne, no date), 2.

11a.1 "I would play diamonds"; in Jules Verne, *Le Tour du monde en quatre-vingts jours* (Lausanne, no date), 259.

the necessary speed. In the end, there remains the heart of the woman in India who is saved right before she tries to throw herself on her husband's funeral pyre — and we as well come to realize that "isn't this more than enough reward for going around the world?" "But "what had the journey brought him?" (Verne 230), meaning he who, as the text never tires of repeating, circles the world like a clock in order to win the bet at the last second and despite his own miscalculation, since the Earth has continued to spin eastward and thus allowed him to gain a day. "One ends up saving 24 hours, the last *coup de théâtre*, in order to make the last turn towards home possible, but at the cost of having to travel 24,000 miles" (Butcher 3).

The irony of the story is that it is in fact the posting of the marriage banns, and the logic of the heart that accompanies them, that makes the mechanical traveler aware of the inexactness of his calculations. In particular, he prefers to spend his time on the journey playing whist, indifferent to the multifaceted impressions to be taken in, or even the many problems that arise. Only his tireless and sometimes overzealous servant Passepartout and the lovely young widow Aounda can rouse him. Otherwise, he moves along "on his scientifically calculated orbit around the world, without bothering about the asteroids gravitating around him" (Verne 97)—he himself being an eccentric in his own right. As a "perfectly regulated piece of machinery," he does not let himself be bothered by "the rolling or pitching of the ship" (Verne 39).

And what existed at the beginning of the journey? Phileas Fogg, who apparently had already traversed the entire world, "at least in spirit" (since in the present he spends three days mechanically reading three newspapers), which raises the theme of the world having shrunk. Fogg's wager is above all the result of his calculated trust in the new order of space, and over the course of almost three months results in little change to his exceedingly ordered life. In the end the heart wins, and despite the money having come up short. His fortune is saved and a heart is won in the process. The new systems are in working order.

Stopover

Jules Verne's famous text exists as a caesura in the history of room travel. From it going forward, many room and mini journeys take their shape from *Around the World in 80 Days*. Hardly any journey can be undertaken without recalling this text. And often it is used as travel reading. Yet more important is that Phileas Fogg is perhaps the last traveler who in circling the Earth can still be certain of finding, amid all the strangeness of the lands he visits, an order to things—even if it is only superficial in nature. The world has indeed shrunk and the far-off has long since lost its allure; yet the traveler commands an attitude of the *désinvolture* (carefreeness),

11a.2.1, 11a2.2, 11a.2.3 Stereophotography of a production of Verne's novel; author's collection.

because the world in a literal sense is an orderly, highly organized, stable, dense space of the mind.

The same is true of the room traveler up until this point, for the room traveler explores an ordered world. And even when, at first, the journey suspends his habits for a certain time, these are reaffirmed even more firmly and emphatically at the end. Room journeys serve the exploration of our own habitus, which of necessity remains hidden to our own gaze, and only through this trick of travel can be made visible. Room journeys also serve the exploration and affirmation of order. Frequently, such order appears only with these journeys, and only through the unique new perspective does it become apparent. Yet all journeys up until Verne's mathematically precise circling of the Earth are explorations of order and ultimately offer stability. It is a dense world that is served up to the eye: a world without gaps, an existence without cracks, a life without fissures. And the little facilitations that these room journeys offer represent the exploration of a space without gaps that facilitates the traveler as well. The journey is a type of communication with a space to which the traveler knows he is connected. For the first time, with the character of Des Esseintes from Joris-Karl Huysmans's À rebours (Against Nature), who was one of the first to draw from Jules Verne, this highly ordered constellation is made to seem fragile. With this comes a profound sense of destabilization that is henceforth true for all journeys: the more that space shrinks and draws back into a room, even into a black box, the more any sense of orientation or order is lost in the world that exists within one's own four walls. Even if, with the help of the computer, the world can be traversed visually through Google Earth, and through other Google searches an endless train of information, libraries, and photo galleries is at the ready, this does not mean that the traveler experiences this world as orderly — but rather the opposite: navigating through the World Wide Web is not forward movement through a homogeneous space, in a contained medium, but rather a navigation from site to site, from link to link, from fissure to fissure, the surfing of waves that exist only for a short while. More to the point: before Phileas Fogg all room travelers are swimmers; after him they are surfers. The medium through which they move changed. And yet once more: "Raise the anchor! It is time!" (Baudelaire 261).

Travel Reading

Baudelaire, Charles. "The Voyage." In *The Flowers of Evil & Paris Spleen*. Trans. William H. Crosby. Brockport, NY, 1991.

Barthes, Roland. *Mythologies*. Trans. Annette Lavers. New York, 1972.

Butcher, William. *Verne's Journey to the Centre of the Self: Space and Time in the Voyages extraordinaires*. London, 1990.

Perec, Georges. "Species of Space." In *"Species of Space" and Other Writings*. Trans. John Sturrock. New York, 1997. 1–91.

Raymond, François. "Tours du monde et tours du texte: Procédés verniens, procédés rousseliens." *La Revue des lettres modernes*, nos. 456–61, 1976. (= *Jules Verne I: Le tour du monde*. Ed. François Raymond. 67–88.)

Renard, Maurice. "Le voyage immobile." In *Ailleurs et demain a vingt ans*. Paris, 1990. 27–71 (First published in 1909.)

Tadié, Jean-Yves. *Regarde, de tous les yeux, regarde*. Paris, 2005.

Verne, Jules. *Around the World in 80 Days*. Trans. Michael Glencross. New York, 2004.

Peregrinations

A curious land, drowned in the mists of our North, it might be called the Orient of the Occident, the China of Europe, so fervently and capriciously has fantasy indulged itself there, so patiently and persistently has it been given luster by a cunning and delicate vegetation.

Baudelaire, 371

Time to go home.

Huysmans, 129

"'Huysmans,'" notes Daniel Grojnowski in his commentary on *À rebours*, "means 'Houseman' in Dutch" (Grojnowski 55). Joris-Karl Huysmans, *this man of the house*, who like his character Des Esseintes sought a life within his work, and within his life a refuge, a house in which he could feel at home, described within this novel a space in which one cannot remain, and yet which is designed for just that. Each attempt to remain in this space results in a journey. Every pause turns immediately into an entry into imaginary worlds. And every sensory perception threatens to become a hallucination, nervous disorder, or a nightmare. Huysmans's room journey in *À rebours* transforms the security of the interior into first a pleasing and then a threatening space of inevitable exile. The room journey neither leads to nor opens up any paradise, but rather plays out the expulsion from it ever anew. It is not a conscious experiment, or a temporary, short-term exception, but rather an inevitable and involuntary thwarting of every attempt to achieve it. The room journey instead lasts in perpetuity.

Appearing in 1884, À rebours is one of those books that polarized people from the very start and still does so today. It's a book with hardly any plot, but instead countless and for the most part subtly inserted references to classical and contemporary literature and art — a book, indeed the book of decadence; in addition, it advances a specific theory about the decline of cultures in regard to their literary production, whose proponent indeed accepts the authors of these phases only on aesthetic terms. It is a book that demarcates an artistic paradise while at the same time expelling its inhabitants, though not before savoring them; while in the end it's also a book that delineates a strictly secular religion whose cult of beauty is served by sundry objects from deconsecrated churches used for newly adopted purposes, and which more than twenty years later would provide the author, who had long since converted to Catholicism, with what he described as an open window through which to flee the surroundings that had begun to suffocate him (Huysmans, Vorwort, 30, 45). The windows in Des Esseintes's house in Fontenay-aux-Roses, however, remain for the most part shut and the rooms stifling. The interior is arranged such that it is not disturbed by the outside world and only expresses its inhabitant's aesthetic preferences. In this way the bibliophile Des Esseintes allows the walls of his home to shut like a book "with rough- or flat-grained Moroccan and calves' leather," which nonetheless is dyed orange for perceptual and psychological reasons, while the windows, whose panes are covered with the bottoms of colored bottles, only allow in muted light from the outside. The newly designed rooms of the dwelling are described in À rebours, as in Edmond de Goncourt's La Maison d'un artiste, object by object, collection by collection, picture by picture, and also book by book. The space of

12.0 Objects among which Gustave Moreau lived; in Peter Hahlbrock, *Gustave Moreau oder Das Unbehagen in der Natur* (Berlin, 1976), illus. 7.

the home should comprise a purely artistic artificiality whose history of art and literature incorporates the proclivities of its inhabitant and provides him with a synesthetic abundance of meaning. Thus, just as his favorite artist Gustave Moreau lives in his home in Paris unnoticed by his neighbors and contemporaries, and through his art turns it into his own space—today his residence, in which some paintings are so large that they simply cannot fit through the doors or windows, is a museum that, as then, still provides the peculiar feeling of being cut off from its surrounding neighborhood—so Des Esseintes's house in Fontenay-aux-Roses is meant to become a refuge from time and space—in which, of course, we find paintings by Moreau as well. Charles Baudelaire's prose poem "N'Importe où Hors du Monde" ("Anywhere Out of the World"), which lies on a communion plate (which in turn like many of the furnishings comes from a church, but now is used for the purposes of a new cult), represents in short how Des Esseintes thinks of his house.

"Nature . . . has had her day" (Huysmans 22); now it should be replaced by culture, indeed by the artificial. The same goes for society, which Des Esseintes renounces in all forms. Even the "cul-

12.1 Gustave Moreau, *Italian Memories*; in Peter Hahlbrock, *Gustave Moreau oder Das Unbehagen in der Natur* (Berlin, 1976), illus. 16.

tured plants" that he buys, since the room is indeed too stifling, are so cultured that one can hardly recognize them as plants. They are "natural flowers that . . . look like fakes" (Huysmans 83), "depraved, unhealthy species" (Huysmans 88) that thereby demonstrate, through the artistry of the grower, that they can outwit evolution and leap over centuries thanks to art. The flowers thus artificially, as well as artistically, outdo nature.

After a debauched social life carried out with pleasure, Des Esseintes the aristocrat had arranged, as described in the history of this particular space, to sell his family's castle in order to move into the refuge of his Thébaïde in a Parisian suburb that was nonetheless still reachable by train from Paris, yet far enough away from the train station that he wouldn't be disturbed by the bustle and traffic. "Once he had cut himself off from contemporary life" (Huysmans 50) and "had to live on his own" (Huysmans 70), he inhabits the ground floor of his new house, placing the upper floors at the disposal of his domestic servants, who walk around in bedroom slippers so as not to disturb him with the sounds of their going back and forth. He sets up room after room according to his wishes and arranges his daily routine like that of a monk without any religious responsibilities. Cut off from the outside world, the house is turned into a space of aesthetic predilection, into a work of art, albeit one that also transforms Des Esseintes's life into the same. "His apartment looks like a dark chamber that reveals the center of interiority" (Grojnowski 57). Yet life does not wish to be transformed into art alone. The body resists being transformed into art and artifice and fights against it with ever-new organic, physiological, and neuronal ailments. The text of the story reads like a travel account of Des Esseintes's Thébaïde, traveling from room to room by moving, on the one hand, from one precious item to another, but also through the accompanying neuroses, hallucinations, delusions, stomach disorders, fevers, nervous breakdowns, and nervous ailments of its inhabitant. Each room then represents a particular disturbance of the mind, speaks to a particular sensory organ, and leads as a result to a specific organic-psychological ailment: sometimes it's the air, sometimes the colors, then other times the literature or the taste; or Des Esseintes sees or smells something that is not there, yet still dominates everything, while other times daydreams or nightmares consume him, or he sees things double or simply out of focus. The stimulation of the collected valuables takes over the organism of Des Esseintes the room traveler, who in the course of the story remains for the most part in a single room and soon is no longer capable of walking around his home. Each of his sensory organs suffers some kind of collapse at least once over the course of his journey through his home, and some suffer the same more than once. The marvel of aesthetic synesthesia, which indeed in the avant-garde represents a paradigm of aesthetic theory, also leads to a multiple overstimulation of the sensory organs. As a result, the peregrination through the house slows until finally it comes to a complete standstill.

The symbol of slowness is the turtle. In Walter Benjamin's *Arcades Project*, this brings to mind the speed of the *flâneur*, who sometimes walks along with a turtle. In *À rebours*, Des Esseintes in fact finds, right in Paris, in a pool near the Palais Royal, a turtle, which seems through its slow movement ideally suited to help the colors of an Oriental rug that he bought stand out more vividly. Yet the turtle in its natural guise is not enough in itself: Des Esseintes has its shell painted with a gold glaze and attaches gemstones to it, thus turning it into a work of art. Yet once it's decked out in this manner, the turtle "refus[es] to budge" (Huysmans 44), and has to be dragged from room to room until it finally relents. Out of its pond and turned into a furnished object, it cannot survive.

The pond and the aquarium appear several times in the text. Frequently, maritime metaphors are used to describe Des Esseintes's room journey — or just their domesticated transformation into aquariums. Indeed, the text ends with a maritime metaphor. In the meantime, the voyager finds himself turned into a galley slave on a brig, having lost his zeal for any kind of pleasure trip. During his journey through his house, by the time he reaches the dining room, which indeed resembles a ship's cabin, it has turned into a ship: "He could then imagine himself between-decks in a brig, and gazed inquisitively at some ingenious mechanical fishes driven by clockwork, which moved backwards and forwards behind the port-hole window and got entangled in artificial seaweed. At other times, while he was inhaling the smell of tar which had been introduced into the room before he entered it, he would examine a series of colour-prints on the walls, such as you see in packet-boat offices and Lloyd's agencies, representing steamers bound for Valparaiso and the River Plate, alongside framed notices giving the itineraries of the Royal Mail Steam Packet Line and the Lopez and Valéry Companies, as well as the freight charges and ports of call of the transatlantic mail-boats" (Huysmans 20). And when such

12.2 Room inside the Musée Gustave Moreau; in Peter Hahlbrock, *Gustave Moreau oder Das Unbehagen in der Natur* (Berlin, 1976), illus. 17.

information overload makes him tired, he simply turns away from the imagined life of far-off ships and harbors to literature, reading Edgar Allan Poe's *The Narrative of Arthur Gordon Pym*, which he has had printed on its own special paper. Next to the dining room door he has various maritime objects, ranging from fishing poles to sailcloth to cork buoys and nets, to further transform the apartment into a ship. The room journey is turned into an imaginary journey to distant seas, even if it only crosses the endless distance of the interior while at the same time frustrates Des Esseintes's desire to ease the troubled sea of images roiling inside him. "By this means he was able to enjoy quickly, almost simultaneously, all the sensations of a long sea-voyage, without ever leaving home; the pleasure of moving from place to place, a pleasure which in fact exists only in recollection of the past and hardly ever in the experience of the present, this pleasure he could savour in full and in comfort, without fatigue or worry, in this cabin whose deliberate disorder, impermanent appearance and makeshift appointments corresponded fairly closely to the flying visits he paid it and the limited time he gave his meals" (Huysmans 21).

When Des Esseintes is tired of the multiple impressions of this room journey, he having become a "traveler suffering from sea-sickness" (Huysmans 152) who wants to escape the stifling air of the interior, he then plans a journey to London. Just as Poe's story lies at the ready in his dining room in order to transform the world about him, this initiates the journey, but with a different literary model: Des Esseintes leaves his house as an Englishman, specifically as Phileas Fogg from Jules Verne's novel *Around the World in 80 Days*. *À rebours* alludes to Verne's novel explicitly, and is in fact a parody of it: Des Esseintes's clothing, as well as his luggage and even the time of departure,* link to Verne's Phileas Fogg, whose name would even seem to remind us of the change in weather, as if the horrible rain on precisely the day of departure has been transformed into a "brackish varnish" that covers the sky and blankets both it and the earth with "countless filaments." The weather is already a harbinger of what he can expect in London. Yet Des Esseintes never arrives there — or perhaps he does, since for him Paris becomes London, and with each glass of alcohol Dickens's characters come more alive and the rooms are transformed. "He settled down comfortably in this London of the imagination, happy to be indoors, and believing for a moment that the dismal hootings of the tugs by the bridge behind the Tuileries were coming from boats on the Thames" (Huysmans 124). The train leaves without him, and he submits himself to his existence as a room traveler — but now with new reasons and experiences: "When you come to think of it," he thus says, "I've seen and felt all that I wanted to see

* "While the train in *Around the World in 80 Days* leaves Charing Cross at 8:45, the one in *À rebours* leaves the Saint-Lazare train station at 8:50" (Grojnowski 101).

and feel. I've been steeped in English life ever since I left home, and it would be madness to risk spoiling such unforgettable experiences by a clumsy change of locality" (Huysmans 129).

The recourse to Dickens also bears witness to another subtext of this particular kind of flight: Gérard de Nerval's story "Les Nuits d'octobre" ("October Nights"), which appeared in 1852 in five installments in the magazine *L'Illustration*. In this story there is also a text by Dickens, a cityscape titled "La Clef de la rue" ("The Key of the Street"), published in *Revue Britannique*, which provides the narrator with a space in which to imagine and make connections. Here as there the protagonists miss the train; here as there they commence instead strange wanderings through Paris; here as there it's about the displacement of a literary tradition: while in *À rebours* Huysmans seeks to set himself apart from naturalistic literature (which has to do in no small part with his disagreement with Émile Zola at the time the novel was published), Nerval is more interested in literary realism. Here the narrator discovers Dickens's story after he has missed the train and utilizes it as a theoretical guide for a journey through the night and the various nether regions of Paris at night. Along with this is the continual question of what it might mean to write a realistic story. "October Nights" is really an experiment in traveling through an allegedly familiar Paris to ascertain how such a city with all its detail, and through its unique as well as everyday places, can be read and presented. In Nerval's text, as in Huysmans's, the familiar reverts to the unfamiliar, the threatening, and the strange. Here as there the journey through the near-at-hand has an *open end* that is at the same time a dead end. "Nerval's experience of the city," Karlheinz Stierle thus sums up, "is symbolized by 'pérégination.' Just as *flânerie* moves through a familiar surround and always only in principle reckons with the familiar through surprise, pérégination involves the journey into the strange and unfamiliar. Nerval's peregrinations are journeys into the strange and unfamiliar of the near-at-hand, into the bottomless strange realities of the city that divest one of knowledge and consciousness" (Stierle 686).

Travel Reading

Baudelaire, Charles. "Invitation to the Voyage." In *Flowers of Evil & Paris Spleen*. Trans. William H. Crosby. Brockport, NY, 1991.

Grojnowski, Daniel. *J.-K. Huysmans, "À Rebours."* Paris, 1996.

Huysmans, Joris-Karl. *À Rebours (Against Nature)*. Trans. Robert Baldick. New York, 2003.

———. Vorwort. "Zwanzig Jahre nach dem Roman geschrieben." In *Gegen den Strich*. Trans. Hans Jacob. Zürich, 1981. 25–52.

Nerval, Gérard de. "Les Nuits d'octobre [1852]." In *Werke*, vol. 2. Munich, 1988. 455–99.

Stierle, Karlheinz. *Der Mythos von Paris: Zeichen und Bewußtsein der Stadt*. Munich, 1998.

Travels with a Room

This filthy rich man, who has had built for himself the most luxurious travel trailer possible will during the time of his life remain the strongest disparager, and the biggest detractor of real travel.

Breton, in Grössel, *Raymond Roussel*, 97

The travel trailer, which in the mid-1930s suddenly filled the highways, had in its early years almost consistently descriptive names, such as "Prairie Schooner," or "Yosemite," "Overlander," "Winnebago," "Apache," "Wagoneer," "Nomad," "Carri-Lite," "Landyacht," and "Terra Cruiser." Built on the model of the gypsy or circus wagon, one could combine being "Always Home" with mobility and hominess: "The car grants us *travel*, the camping trailer a feeling of *home*" (Berger 10). Travel trailers are "mobile homes" (Berger 86) that provide the feel of a familiar surround while on a journey, and which allow us, no matter where we travel, "to maintain the *feel of home*" (Berger 17).

What today seems like one of the most philistine forms of travel, and which led to all kinds of camping grounds both at home and abroad literally turning into new settlements of stationary mobile homes that are only occupied during vacations, and yet can be broken down and hauled off at any time, all this—believe it or not—has a historical model that comes from the highpoint of the avant-garde. In 1925, Raymond Roussel, who is unquestionably one of the most erratic and enigmatic figures of twentieth-century French literature, and who still poses puzzles that cannot be solved by numerous prominent critics such as Michel Foucault, Michel Leiris, Alain Robbe-Grillet, or even André Breton, had his "Roulotte" built—a van nine meters long and 2.3 meters wide, in which he traveled from Paris to Rome in December 1926 in order to have an audience with the pope and to pay a visit to Benito Mussolini. It seems obvious that Roussel's touring car was inspired by Jules Verne, who was one of his favorite authors, and from whose character Phileas Fogg he had taken on the mindset, in matters of travel, of imperturbable *désinvolture*, as Ernst Jünger probably would say. What's not clear is whether Verne's story "César Cascabel" is the godfather of his inspiration, as Philippe G. Kerbellec asserts, or indeed, as François Caradec argues, it is Verne's *Maison à vapeur* (*The Steam House*) (Caradec 296). His caravan caused such a stir that even in 1926 there appeared in the popular magazine *L'Illustration* an article that described this nomadic home, and also provided photos for the eyes of the interested reader.

That Roussel had such a touring car built is not at all surprising, for his version of travel accounts also demonstrates that his extensive and detailed descriptions of his travels are not focused on the far but rather on the near. The almost two thousand verses of *La Vue* are nothing more than a description of an "enclosed view" (Roussel, *La Vue*, 9), more precisely the image of a beach that is inserted into the top half of a pen and that moves back and forth. Even today, we can purchase such pens in seaside spots and other tourist places, and then watch a ship move from left to right and from right to left through imaginary waves inside the pen, or watch a penguin bob up and down amid icebergs. "A view," writes Annie Le Brun, "that is as new as it is paradoxical, in which simply the relationship between the near and the far is revolutionized" (Le

TOURISME PRÉCURSEUR

LA VILLA NOMADE

Au lendemain de la première victoire de la Marne, comme on demandait au maréchal Joffre, alors général, quels seraient ses projets après la guerre, le grand soldat ne se fit pas prier pour avouer, avec sa bonhomie coutumière, qu'il ne faisait pas un autre rêve que de courir la France, à petites journées, par le délicieux réseau de routes liquides que forment ses canaux, à bord d'une péniche aménagée pour constituer un chalet flottant. Et, la paix venue, le vainqueur des grandes journées de septembre 1914 se donna le délassement qu'il avait dit.

On ne saurait concevoir, en effet, un mode de déplacement plus agréable et plus fertile en sensations constamment renouvelées que celui qui permet de « cueillir le jour » au gré d'une fantaisie vagabonde, sous le ciel qui aura séduit, au sein du paysage qui sera un enchantement des yeux, sans renoncer néanmoins à une seule de ses habitudes, en continuant à jouir de tous les avantages du home familier, en s'assurant, enfin, la satisfaction unique du voyageur sans quitter son « chez soi ».

Novateur en matière de tourisme, comme il l'est hardiment en littérature, M. Raymond Roussel, l'auteur d'*Impressions d'Afrique* et de *Locus Solus*, a repris, en la perfectionnant, l'idée du maréchal. Il n'est fait établir, sur ses plans, une automobile géante, mesurant 9 m. sur 2 m. 30, et comprenant par suite de dispositions ingénieuses, un salon, un studio, une chambre à coucher, une salle de bains et même un véritable petit dortoir pour le personnel composé de trois hommes : deux chauffeurs et un valet.

Le châssis Saurer à frein moteur de cette villa roulante, ou de cette « roulotte automobile », comme la désigne trop modestement son propriétaire et inventeur, peut observer la coquette allure de 40 kilomètres à l'heure. La carrosserie, œuvrée par

La « roulotte automobile » dans le jardin de la propriété
de M. Raymond Roussel, à Neuilly.

Un appartement à transformation : le salon-chambre à coucher
sous son aspect de salon, orné de glaces, éclairé par de larges baies
et muni de fauteuils profonds.

Une autre physionomie de jour du salon-chambre à coucher :
le studio où toutes les commodités ont été prévues pour aider
à la méditation féconde et faciliter le travail.

Le salon-chambre à coucher disposé pour la nuit en vue
du troisième rôle qu'il est appelé à remplir : celui d'asile
moelleux du sommeil.

La salle de bains, dernier mot de l'art de l'installation sur un
minimum de surface et de l'hygiène bien comprise, c'est-à-dire
alliant le luxe à la simplicité.

Le « quartier » du personnel, le jour ; le soir, trois couchettes
à rabattement en font un dortoir.

Lacoste, est une merveille, moins encore par l'élégance de haut cachet de sa ligne extérieure que par son miraculeux agencement intérieur. C'est ainsi que la chambre à coucher se transforme, le jour venu, en salon ou en studio, tour à tour, et que la partie avant de la voiture devient, pour le campement du soir, au moyen de couchettes à rabattement, une petite chambrée où trois hommes peuvent tenir à l'aise et disposent même d'un lavabo.

Il y a le chauffage électrique et une cheminée à gaz d'essence. Le chauffe-bain fonctionne au gaz d'essence. La décoration est signée de Maple. Le mobilier a été prévu d'une façon tellement faite pour répondre à tous les besoins qu'il comprend jusqu'à un coffre-fort Fichet. Une installation de T. S. F., dotée des derniers perfectionnements, achève de faire de la « villa nomade », qui peut se compléter d'une cuisine-remorque, très probablement, la plus belle automobile du monde. M. Raymond Roussel y a déjà accompli, au cours du dernier été, une randonnée de 3.000 kilomètres à travers la Suisse et l'Alsace, couvrant chaque jour une étape.

Il est à penser que ce véritable précurseur fera école. M. Raymond Roussel a ouvert au grand tourisme une voie nouvelle, car sa formule concilie heureusement deux tendances maîtresses de l'époque : la passion du mouvement, qui est une survivance de l'esprit d'aventure, et l'amour du confort.

Des jours viendront où les « villas nomades » courront nombreuses sur les routes du monde, renouvelant dans une forme humaine et pour le plaisir raffiné de leurs occupants, l'ère révolue des peuples pasteurs et l'époque, qui achève de s'éteindre, des Zingaris errants, amants impénitents de la nature, du grand air et de la liberté sans entraves sous le ciel.

13.0   Raymond Roussel's "Villa Nomade"; in "Tourisme précurseur: LA VILLA NOMADE," *L'Illustration*, February 26, 1926.

Brun 29). The same is true for "La Source" and "Le Concert," which likewise at some point take their inspiration from an image and never let go of it: the label of a bottle of mineral water or vignette on a sheet of stationery serves as the starting point or end point of the abundant description in the text. "In truth," writes Michel Foucault, who devoted an entire book to Roussel, "few works can travel less, are more immobile than those of Raymond Roussel: nothing in them moves except for these internal motions predetermined by the enclosed space of the machines: nothing is out of place; everything sings of the perfection of a peace that vibrates within itself and whose every figure shifts position only to better indicate its place and immediately return to it" (Foucault 78). Roussel describes things as if they were speaking entities, a clear-eyed view tied only to words and which disregards the things themselves. He develops with imperturbable obstinacy ever-new methods of description that consist of new rules, standards, and internal points of reference without taking into account any possible approach to description. His passion is for the continual building of patterns and structures, interferences and construed relations, from superficial and artificial associations between words. Raymond Roussel construes an ever-thicker evolving network of words that at no time seeks to describe a visible reality, or ever betrays a mimetic impulse, while in the end the hope is that the network is woven together tightly enough to take in the entire world.* Foucault called this new speech "the solar language": this in fact can be found in the magnifying "lens of La Vue, enveloping men, words, things, faces, dialogues, thoughts, gestures, all displayed without any reticence or secret" (Foucault 163). We could also call it the language of the stars: Roussel was in fact a fer-

* "That which Roussel sees is not the interior, but rather an enclosure, which though it recedes endlessly, never fails to have an influence on the outer in order to encompass it entirely. It's as if the eyeball were to have only the goal of encompassing the entire globe" (Le Brun 30 f.).

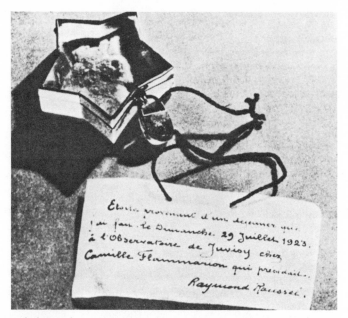

13.1 The biscuit that Raymond Roussel took away from a lunch with Camille Flammarion and had preserved in a glass star; in François Caradec, *Vie de Raymond Roussel* (Paris, 1997), illus. 46.

vent follower of Camille Flammarion, who at the end of the nineteenth and the beginning of the twentieth centuries succeeded at bridging the (completely shameless) gulf between astronomy and spiritualism. From his visit with Flammarion on July 29, 1923, at the Meudon observatory, Roussel brought home a biscuit that he enclosed in a glass star to protect it like a relic.[†] Already in 1872, Flammarion imagined in his novel *Lumen* for a character of the same name a trip to outer space that, just by sheer will, could pass through endless distance. According to the postmortem perception of beings composed of light, the entire world is transformed into will and imagination in stories whose historical locale depends on

[†] See, by way of comparison, also the notebook of Michel Leiris: p. 40 in the original pagination and p. 137 in the printed edition.

the particular stellar position of the observer. Lumen's cognitive capabilities owe a lot to simple physical laws, and above all to the phenomenon of the speed of light. When a beam of light, or so says the being of light to his skeptical listener, needs a certain amount of time to pass through space, then all it needs is to move sufficiently far away from the Earth to be observed in both a time-delayed and a *simultaneous* manner: "So it only requires a sufficiently piercing power of sight to witness historical and geological events that have long since passed. Could not one so gifted, in that case, see the Deluge, the Garden of Eden, Adam and . . ." (Flammarion 34). And this "and" can be elaborated upon by a posthistorical remark: "The past of the star *is*, scientifically speaking, the present of the observer. . . . It is not the actual condition of the heavens that is visible, but their past history" (Flammarion 22). In space the present is transformed into history and history into the present. Beyond the threshold of death there awaits for the deceased a simulacrum of this world. The universe is an inexhaustible archive of images of the Earth in which all events can be called up. The observer can "surf" between different eras of what has occurred, depending on whether he moves away slower or faster than the speed of light. If he moves faster than light, then history runs backward; if he moves slower, history's film fast-forwards. What for Flammarion is a visual-luminous materialization in ether appears in Roussel as something linguistic-constellative. Images become words, stars become symbols, words become constellations that imitate the distant constellations beyond.

Roussel revealed some of his methods in his text *How I Have Written Certain of My Books* — and these are the most famous examples of such a principle of construction. One consists of placing two nearly homophonic, but also semantically different sentences at the beginning and end of a text. His task as a writer is then to imagine a link between these two sentences and to write

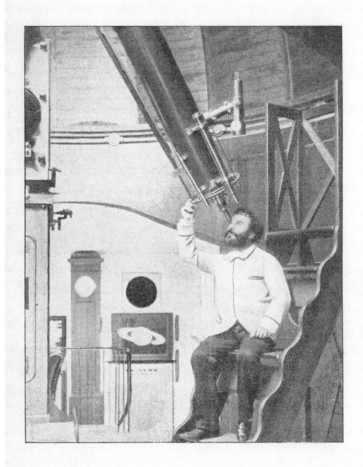

UNE OBSERVATION A L'AIDE DE L'ÉQUATORIAL.

13.2 Juvisy's observatory; in Camille Flammarion, *Promenades dans les étoiles* (Paris, 1910), 3.

it out.[†] Given the complexity of Roussel's methods, it's no wonder that he does not stay with a simple narrative linkage, though he indeed sees all linguistic obstacles as solvable tasks and observed *contraintes* (constraints), taking up a concept of the Oulipo Group, whose best-known members were Georges Perec, Raymond Queneau, and Italo Calvino, all of whom owe much to Roussel. In *How I Wrote Certain of My Books*, Roussel also raises the question of travel, he appearing at a minimum to have been an avid traveler: "It seems apt that I should mention here a rather curious fact. I have traveled a great deal. Notably in 1920–21, I traveled around the world, by way of India, Australia, New Zealand, the Pacific archipelagos, China, Japan, and America. . . . I already knew the most important countries of Europe, Egypt, and all of North Africa, and later I visited Constantinople, Asia Minor, and Persia. Now, from all these travels I never took anything for my books. It seems to me that this is worth mentioning, since it clearly shows just how much imagination accounts for everything in my work" (Roussel, *How I Wrote*, 20). Indeed, there's more. Michel Leiris reports in an essay on Roussel: "While traveling around the world by sea, Roussel received a letter from a close friend in which she tells him how jealous she was that he could see so many marvelous sights, such as the sunsets, which must be so lovely! He answered her that he had seen none of them, since he had been working in his cabin and hadn't left it for days" (Leiris, "Der Reisende," 90).[§] Roussel, it is reported (see Foucault 175), withdrew to his room during his travels, be they by boat, by train, or in his touring car,

[†] The most famous — and also cited by Roussel — example is: "Les lettres du blanc sur les bandes du vieux pillard/billard" ("The white letters on the edge of the old billiards table," and correspondingly "The letters of a white-skinned man about the old pillager's gangs").

[§] "Raymond Roussel travels in a type of 'mobile dwelling' around the world. He casts not a single glance outwards. He remains inside, pleased to simply be on the move, rather than looking at the landscapes passing by" (Leuwers 111).

making sure to close the curtains carefully in order to not be disturbed by anything from outside — and wrote.** And even though he used all means of forward motion and, like Phileas Fogg, none was too expensive for him, language was really his only means of transport. Alain Robbe-Grillet correctly stresses that with Raymond Roussel there is only the surface nature of the words, and that nothing or no secret lies behind them, even when all his texts revolve around secrets — nor are they even about the epidermis of the globe, which he constantly traveled, for the surface of language is what replaces it. And so Roussel traveled with dictionaries and encyclopedias (Leiris, *Roussel & Co.*, 10/81).

Constantly under way, it's still true "that Roussel never traveled in any real sense. For it seems probable that he never devoted a single moment to being a tourist, that the external world never impeded upon the universe that he carried inside himself, and that of the lands he visited he only saw what he brought to them ahead of time: elements that only corresponded to the universe that he inhabited. . . . Just as he did in his touring car, Roussel traveled 'without ever leaving his dwelling for a single day'" (Leiris, "Der Reisende," 92 f.). Roussel, we can surmise, had his "Roulotte" built in order to travel and not have to leave his room. His ideal, it appears, is to bring together the far and the near, to be able to travel far and yet be able to stay right in his room. Should he not wish to cross the threshold, then the threshold itself can travel far.

Just as Jules Verne and Camille Flammarion were for Raymond Roussel authors immersed in the fantastic, so Roussel was for Michel Leiris — and there are many biographical coincidences to support it[tt] — a benchmark who also had consequences for his writing

---

** "While he was traveling on a ship across the seas, he realized that while working, he had not left his cabin in days. When he arrived in Peking, after a short visit to the city he returned to his cabin once again" (Leiris, *Roussel & Co.*, p. 4 of the notebook and p. 74 of the transcription).

[tt] Such as the fact that Leiris tried to commit suicide the day Roussel died.

as well as his travels. In addition to Leiris writing "Der Reisende und sein Schatten" ("The Traveler and His Shadow"), one of the definitive texts about Roussel's peculiar strategies for traveling, among his papers is a notebook titled *Cahier Raymond Roussel* that probably was meant to serve as a collection of materials for the planned biography that Leiris wanted to take up after his return from the Dakar-Djibouti mission, which Roussel helped finance (Leiris, *Roussel & Co.*, 9). Right before Leiris left for Africa on an ethnological expedition, which he later used for *Phantom Afrika*, one of the most important ethnographic texts of the first half of the twentieth century, he wrote to Roussel and asked him for a copy of his as yet unpublished book *Nouvelles Impressions d'Afrique* (Leiris, *Roussel & Co.*, 292, letter from April 11, 1931), which again really does read like a travel account, though not of real landscapes but rather of "photographed (i.e. artificial) landscapes, . . . such that between him and nature it is as if there exists a plethora of screens" (Leiris, *Roussel & Co.*, notebook p. 66/transcription p. 177). It appears that Leiris did not want to leave for Africa without reading Roussel's book — even if it had nothing to do with an eyewitness account of the dark continent. He also wrote a letter on February 10, 1931, in which he admitted, "The best years of my life were those between six and eleven. If travel has such a powerful pull for me now, then it's because it is the best means to bring back this remarkable childhood as a grownup. That material and moral support for a journey tackled by me has come from the author of numerous books that have brought me great joy since childhood, this is for me an occurrence whose particular value you can only guess at through what I have reported to you" (Leiris, *Roussel & Co.*, 290). For Roussel *was* one of the important figures of Leiris's childhood, and he was indeed a friend of his father's and could imitate him perfectly. Moreover, Leiris's reconstruction of Roussel's poetics, in which he works out a method that, with the help

13.3 Michel Leiris, who in 1932 wrote the first account of the Dakar-Djibouti mission; in Michel Leiris, *Miroir de l'afrique* (Paris, 1996), 84.

of a mythical nominalism, not only battles against death, against which he poses the simulacrum of words, but seeks to create the universe anew,[††] has much to do with his own literary efforts, and not least of all with his diary from the Dakar-Djibouti mission. Leiris's expedition was his own version of Roussel's Africa book, as well as of his particular approach to travel. And thus he writes in 1930 in regard to the Dakar-Djibouti mission in *Documents*, the magazine published by himself, Carl Einstein, and Georges Bataille, a piece that is almost an homage to Roussel: "What strikes me, who during a trip fulfills a number of childhood dreams — by using the best ways and means to succeed at acquiring a lively awareness of things — as if it were a means to battle against aging and death, in which there is certainly plenty of room to encounter thoughts of the passing of time (in which one forgets one's own tentative personality through contact with many obviously very different people), is that I wish . . . that as many of my artistic or literary friends as possible would let go of problems that in the end stem from aesthetic causes or pointless squabbles that develop between different groups, and do like I do, namely not travel as tourists (for that means to travel without a heart, without eyes, and without ears), but rather as ethnologists in order to become more fully human and forget their mediocre 'white manners' (so say some negroes), as well as what they even consider an intellectual 'person' to be" (Leiris, *Roussel & Co.*, 328).

* * *

Some decades later, Martin Scorsese's film *The Aviator* portrayed the multimillionaire Howard Hughes, who made his wealth from

[††] "Nominalism in the magical sense: the word evokes the thing, the dismantling of any sentence leads to the reconfiguration of the universe, the creation of a particular universe that replaces the normal universe" (Leiris, *Roussel & Co.*, notebook p. 20/transcription p. 101).

no less than airplanes, as having withdrawn into a room — or more precisely many rooms, all of which were set up like one another. Hughes spent many months in 1957 in these nearly identical rooms, going from one to another under the cover of darkness without being noticed, lying naked on a bed that was always in the same spot while watching the same movies again and again on a specially installed movie screen, eating the same food over and over, and avoiding all contact with the outside world (Virilio 29 f.). One of these movies, which he apparently watched more than 150 times and which ran as a continuous loop, was *Ice Station Zebra*, which ironically was about an American submarine that passes a long ways under polar ice to reach the remains of a satellite with important footage onboard, and which has crashed near Ice Station Zebra. The submarine floating in the dark of the polar sea, the research station in the icy cold, and the satellite on its lonely orbit — these are three variations of a journey that fascinated Hughes, and from whose images he could not free himself.

Travel Reading

Berger, Hans. *Jachten der Landstraße: Das Buch vom Wohn-Anhänger*. Stuttgart, 2005 (reprint of first edition, 1938).

Caradec, François. *Raymond Roussel*. Paris, 1997.

Flammarion, Camille. *Lumen*. Trans. Brian Stableford. Middletown, 2002.

Foucault, Michel. *Death and the Labyrinth: The World of Raymond Roussel*. Trans. Charles Ruas. New York, 1986.

Hauser, Heinrich. *Fahren und Abenteuer im Wohnwagen*. Stuttgart, 2004 (reprint of first edition, Dresden, 1935).

Kerbellec, Philippe G. *Comment lire Raymond Roussel: Cryptanalyse*. Paris, 1988.

Le Brun, Annie. *Vingt mille lieus sous les mots, Raymond Roussel.* Paris, 1994.

Leiris, Michel. "Lœil de l'ethnographie: A propos de la Mission Dakar-Djibouti." *Documents*, vol. 2, no. 7, 1930.

———. *Miroir de l'Afrique.* Paris, 1996.

———. "Der Reisende und sein Schatten." In *Raymond Roussel, In Havanna: Ein Romanfragment.* Frankfurt am Main, 1984. 88–93. (First published as Michel Leiris. "Le Voyageuer et son ombre." *La Bête noire*, no. 1. April 1935.)

———. *Roussel & Co.* Ed. Jean Jamin. Paris, 1998.

Leuwers, Daniel. "Le Voyage immobile." In Leuwers, *Le voyage immobile.* Saint-Estève, 2001. 103–14.

Roussel, Raymond. "Le Concert." In Roussel, *La Vue.*

———. *How I Wrote Certain of My Books.* Ed. and trans. Trevor Winkfield. Boston, 1995.

———. "La Source." In Rousel, *La Vue.*

———. *La Vue.* Paris, 1963. (First published Paris, 1904.)

———. "Wie ich einige meiner Bücher geschrieben habe." In Hanns Grössel, ed. *Raymond Roussel: Eine Dokumentation.* Munich, 1977. 79–97.

Scorsese, Martin, director. *The Aviator.* 163 min. USA, 2004.

"Tourisme précurseur: LA VILLA NOMADE." *L'Illustration*, February 26, 1926.

Virilio, Paul. *Rasender Stillstand.* Berlin, 1980.

A Cinematic Baedeker

Travel has "nothing to do with having to really journey to far off places. This state is really an inner state. One develops a different relation with the outer world. . . . One need not even leave the room at all."

Balázs, 94

Before you had to leave in order to arrive. Now things arrive before anyone's leaving.

Virilio and Lotringer, 68

"This term was coined by the Russian film-maker Dziga Vertov," so writes Béla Balázs in his epochal book *The Spirit of Film*. "His idea was to make travelogues which lead the spectator not into remote, unknown parts, but to unknown places close by. To use the camera, the *cine-eye*, to eavesdrop on scenes from everyday lives. The most insignificant scenes become meaningful here because, when removed and isolated from their context, they attract our full attention. They become exemplary. *Pars pro toto*: 'This is how life is!' . . . The journey into the world close by follows no route or map, and hence has no form. It produces no coherent sequence of events and no story, and yet what presents itself to us in the image is nonetheless a form of creative writing, a creative experience. For what we are given is not scientific knowledge but impressions

The same impression that moves us so deeply—if we have eyes, nerves and a heart—when we walk through the streets" (Balázs, *The Spirit of Film*, 152–53).

Balázs alludes here solely to Vertov and not at all to Walter Ruttmann, who at roughly the same time devoted himself to a similar undertaking with his film *Berlin, Symphony of a Metropolis*. Vertov's *Der Mann mit der Kamera* has a very comparable structure, since both films show a day in the "life" of a city, and in each of them montage plays a prominent role. In his review of Vertov's film, Siegfried Kracauer differentiated between the two approaches to montage and also evaluated them. While in his view Ruttmann's film is composed almost completely of associations, these are also almost purely formal and therefore result only in the loose order achieved through juxtaposition, whereas "Vertov achieves a more unified sensibility through the binding together of slivers of reality" (Kracauer 248). Although he presents only the visible and everyday reality, "[he] reaches below the surface" and "he breaks through the ostensible, closed-off reality of the collective" (Kracauer 249). Vertov aspires to a new order of things, a new order of life, through his cinematic journeys.

This altered approach, this new perspective on the supposedly familiar near-at-hand, is central to Vertov's films. Whether then Balázs is right in saying that Vertov's journey has "no determined route" and "no form," and also offers no "scientific knowledge" but instead presents more of a kind of poetry that relies on a remarkable compilation of impressions, is doubtful, if we read Vertov's writings on film theory. Important to consider is that Balázs stands Vertov's fundamental intention on its head with his description of Vertov's films as "creative writing" and combinations of "creative experience" that rely not on an objective but rather on a purely subjective context.

Vertov is much more about—to put it scientifically—an analysis of reality that provides the viewer with a new awareness

14.0 Dziga Vertov, *The Man with a Movie Camera*; film still.

through the medium of montage as visual synthesis. As a result, montage in itself can be described as a multilevel process of abstraction and selection, allowing the filmmaker, according to Vertov, "to organize the film pieces wrested from life into a meaningful rhythmic visual order, a meaningful visual phrase, an essence of 'I see'" (Vertov 88). Vertov interprets, as Kracauer states, the coexistence of everyday life, which "year in, year out" continues, and "which he depicts" (Kracauer 248). The cinematic journey through the everyday, which presents to the (Soviet) viewer his own life, aims at a visual "transmission from brain to brain" (Vertov 260). It touches on, so far as we can construe today, the theory of reflexology from the Leningrad School, namely the work of Ivan Pavlov and Vladimir Bechterev, under whom Vertov also studied.

Dziga Vertov's miniature journey aims for a revolution in ways of seeing and also thinking. He himself makes no secret of the revolutionary claims of his films — and that can be understood on

14.1 Dziga Vertov, *The Man with a Movie Camera*; film still.

several levels. All aspects of his cinematic work are about revolution: a revolution in art, in perception, in human beings, and in society. The focus of his films is therefore a thorough view of the quotidian in all its everyday appearances. At no point does Vertov follow a completed script, but rather amid the chaos of phenomena he seeks to formulate an order of appearances. It's therefore essential that he emphatically define the lens in objective fashion, as if it were separate from the human eye. Already in the early manifesto "Kinoki-Umsturz" from 1922, Vertov proclaims this freeing of the camera from any subjugation to the eye, which he thoroughly shares with other theorists of his time, such as Alexander Rodchenko or László Moholy-Nagy. "We therefore take as the point of departure the use of the camera as a kino-eye, more perfect than the human eye, for the exploration of the chaos of visual phenomena that fills space" (Vertov 14–15). However, these visual appearances proceed, according to Vertov's theory, not at all

14.2 Dziga Vertov, *The Man with a Movie Camera*; film still.

chaotically; rather, certain underlying rules and laws exist within them, which it is the task of film, and more specifically montage, to depict. The task, then, is to view the "system of seeming irregularities," and from within it to ascertain and order appearances as a "system of successive movements" (Vertov 15–16). It's about visualizing, thanks to the objectivity attributed to the camera lens, an objective order of appearances and returning it to the human gaze as cinematically organized appearances — or in the words of Vertov, about organizing "details into a montage study" (Vertov 16), which makes possible "an exceptionally fresh and interesting aspect" (Vertov 19). The known world reveals itself through the culmination of the objective as only *apparently* known, and which through cinematic means of transformation can be perceived in different, new forms and whose workings, having been made visible, can be identified. "I decipher in a new way a world unknown to you" (Vertov 18). Film is a visual and, at the same time, experi-

14.3 Dziga Vertov, *The Man with a Movie Camera*; film still.

mental art of deciphering the structures of life: "Life's chaos gradually becomes clear as he observes and shoots. Nothing is accidental. Everything is explicable and governed by law" (Vertov 287).
Through this film logic, Vertov starts with the "influence through
facts as opposed to influence through fiction" (Vertov 77). Through
his cinematic pursuit of truth, he seeks a radical revolution in perception, and through it to arrive at a mindset, or more precisely, a
transition that films should lead us to, namely from appearances
to the unwritten laws of (industrial and social) life, from a theatri-
cal to a cinematic conception of it, and finally from the use of sets
in the film industry to a newly ordered, mounted, and rhythmi-
cally organized chaos of phenomena. He sets forth "the creation
of a fresh perception" (Vertov 18) as a *theoria*. The visual journey through the thicket of everyday phenomena is imagined as a
cinematic-scientific laboratory that implicates the observer in a
complex experimental system, which then returns his everyday

world to him in altered form and prepares him for the revolution. And that's also true for the exploration of a room. Vertov notes in his "artistic visitor's cards," in which he minutely records all his projects, including a "film-phrase which is the room": "First attempt," it says there, "not to show just a room through montage, but rather what it can become or what it could possibly be" (Vertov 2006, 85). That doesn't mean that a film has to reveal a room of the future, as in a science-fiction film, but only that it must show it as *different*. Walter Benjamin, in referring to Vertov, described this transformation of a room as constructive destruction that transforms the passing of the everyday into a journey. "Our bars and city streets, our offices and furnished rooms, our railroad stations and our factories seemed to close relentlessly around us. Then came film and exploded this prison-world with the dynamite of the split second, so that we can set off calmly on journeys of adventure among its widely far-flung debris" (Benjamin 117).

Dziga Vertov sets forth a cinematic exploration of the everyday life of a large city as a travel guide for a visual revolution. He supplies the cinematic counterpart to Sergei Tretyakov, who when asked what he was working on, recorded that he was trying to develop a new kind of Baedeker that would explain to people their altered surroundings (Tretyakov 24). Reading the new world — that is the project on which Vertov, Tretyakov, and also Rodchenko work on. For the last, it was also a matter, like for his friend Vertov, of a revolution in seeing that had no need to ramble off into the distance in order to see a new world, since the near-at-hand itself had not yet been seen and remained undiscovered — and this was ripe for discovery. Rodchenko, like Vertov, undertook visual expeditions into the everyday with the help of a camera to lift the veil from the eyes which tradition had placed over them. "It is wonderful," so Rodchenko notes in his diary from 1927, "to go on expeditions to the North or to Africa, and there photograph new people and new things, and even new nature. Yet what do people do? They photograph with the smoky eyes of a Corot or Rembrandt, with museum eyes, with eyes full of all of art history. . . . Even Africa. Stay home and try to find something completely new" (Gaßner 68).

Travel Reading

Balázs, Béla. "Reisen." In *Ein Baedeker der Seele und andere Feuilletons*. Berlin, 2002. 93–95. (First published in *Der Phantasie-Reiseführer / Das ist ein Baedeker der Seele / Für Sommerfrischler*. Berlin/Vienna/Leipzig, 1925.)

——. "The Spirit of Film." In *Early Film Theory*. Trans. Rodney Livingstone. New York, 2010.

Benjamin, Walter. "The Work of Art in the Age of Its Reproducibility." In *Selected Writings*, vol. 3. Trans. Edmund Jephcott and Harry Zohn. Cambridge, 2002. 101–3.

Dziga Vertov: Die Vertov-Sammlung im Österreichischen Filmmuseum. Eds. Österreichisches Filmmuseum, Thomas Tode, and Barbara Wurm. Vienna, 2006.

Gaßner, Hubertus. *Rodcenko-Fotografien*. Munich, 1982.

Kracauer, Siegfried. "Der Mann mit dem Kinoapparat," from *Kleine Schriften zum Film*. Vol. 2, 1928–31 (In *Werke*. Eds. Inka Mülder-Bach and Ingrid Belke. Vol. 6.2, ed. Inka Mülder-Bach. Frankfurt am Main, 2004). 247–51.

Ruttmann, Walter. *Berlin, die Sinfonie der Großstadt*. Germany, 1927.

Tretjakov, Sergej. *Lyrik, Dramatik, Prosa*. Leipzig, 1972.

Vertov, Dziga. *Kino-Eye: The Writings of Dziga Vertov*. Ed. Annette Mason. Trans. Kevin O'Brien. Berkeley, 1984.

——. *Schriften zum Film*. Munich/Vienna, 1973.

Virilio, Paul, and Sylvère Lotringer. *Pure War*. Trans. Mark Polizotti. New York, 1983.

The Journey to La Défense

As Chateaubriand wrote, "Every man carries within himself a
world made up of all that he has seen and loved; and it is to this
world that he returns incessantly, though he may pass through,
and seem to inhabit, a world quite foreign to it."

Lévi-Strauss, 45–46

We live in a world that we have not yet learned to look at.

Augé, *Non-Places*, 35–36

"Travel and travellers," begins perhaps the most important ethnological book of the present, Claude Lévi-Strauss's *Tristes Tropiques*,
"are two things I loathe — and yet here I am, all set to tell the story
of my expeditions" (Lévi-Strauss 17). Lévi-Strauss sketches an
aporia in which any expedition must emphatically come to terms
with the right of others to exist. While on the one hand the ancient traveler could still discover foreign cultures but was blind
to them, since he was interested not in their cultural but rather
their material treasures, on the other hand today's traveler is con-
fronted with the fact that he remains an "archaeologist of space,
trying in vain to piece together the idea of the exotic with the help
of a particle here and a fragment of debris there" in the pursuit of
"the remains of a reality that has disappeared" (Lévi-Strauss 44),
globalization having also long since taken a toll. Only in memory,

after "twenty years' forgetfulness" (Lévi-Strauss 46), a view opens up for Lévi-Strauss, a new perspective on the journey into the past, which meshes life's journey and the journey of exploration, resulting in a glimpse of the role of the human being in the universe.

"As an ethnologist," writes the anthropologist Marc Augé in reference to Lévi-Strauss, "I don't hate to travel. Yet one's own home is like a micro-society, the core of a society, and a particular culture" (Augé 1985, 24). And so we don't have to roam afar when the pleasure of the ethnologist's gaze is so near at hand. Augé has undertaken an ethnology of the near-at-hand and the everyday in many of his numerous books. The Metro or the amusement park, the spatial layout of a city, real estate ads, or the workings of mass tourism are some of his favorite subjects. On or about July 29, 1984, he began the *Traversée du Luxembourg* (*Traversing the Luxembourg Gardens*), which then appeared as *Ethno-Roman d'une journée française considérée sous l'angle des mœurs de la théorie et du bonheur* (*An Ethnological Novel of a French Day Examined in Light of the Principles of Theory and Happiness*). Augé sought through the applied gaze of the ethnographer to depict the everyday with different, foreign eyes. Just as room journeys of his own interior sought to take in all details, objects, and their narratives with an estranged gaze, so now the traveling gaze takes in ethnological peculiarities and regularities, or the makeup of the present. The room journey or the journey into the near-at-hand of the everyday serves thus as a type of inverted gaze, which Fritz Kramer took as the task of ethnology in general: indeed, while for Kramer the view of the distant was much less about that than it was about the view of the distant and the near, for Augé it is about the experience of alterity, which already is inherent in the everyday and should be just as important as classic ethnographic subjects such as human relations, gift giving, or trade. Even in present-day societies, with their quickening pace and accelerated change in fundamental parameters, excess becoming indeed the norm, there arises the question of alterity, which has enormous consequences for all. This is particularly apparent in certain zones of the everyday that Augé calls *non-lieux*, or non-places. They are places of planning and calculus that the lone individual can only then enter when he has a pass, buys a ticket, or with a recognized credit card pays to enter such a space, in which he immediately forsakes his individuality, and loneliness and conformity become the rule, such as in department stores, subway stations, Disneyland, or tourist sites in which the object of the traveler's contemplation is displaced. "There are spaces in which the individual feels himself to be a spectator without paying much attention to the spectacle. As if the position of spectator were the essence of the spectacle, as if basically the spectator in the position of a spectator were his own spectacle. . . . The traveler's space may thus be the archetype of the *non-place*" (Augé 1995, 86).

On February 22, 1974, Peter Handke set out on a "Journey to La Défense," a journey to one such non-place in Paris. It can be found along with the text that appeared a year earlier, "The Open Secrets of the Technocracy," in the volume *Als das Wünschen noch geholfen hat* (*When Wishing Still Helped*). Handke describes here two journeys: one through the Märkische quarter of Berlin, and a second through the Parisian neighborhood of high-rise apartments and offices known as La Défense, which nonetheless lies only a few subway stations from the heart of the metropolis. Today we can see the gigantic arch that François Mitterrand erected as an architectural monument from the Tuileries, since it is on the same axis as the Arc d'Triomphe on the Champs-Elysées.

Handke's text makes use of his own gaze, as well as that of the stranger's, and describes the neighborhood of office buildings as a kind of negative paradise that displays to the world just what it is. "It was," according to Handke, "like the Promised Land, but not in the sense of Paradise, but rather in the sense that it displayed the condition of the world as remaining forever undisguised and unfabricated" (Handke 35). La Défense no longer defends the pretti-

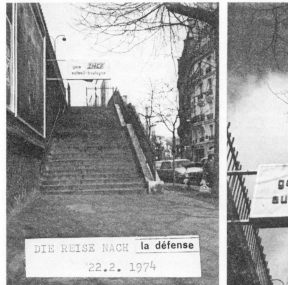

15.0.1, 15.0.2 Peter Handke, *La Défense*; in Peter Handke, "Die Reise nach La Défense," in *Als das Wünschen noch geholfen hat* (Frankfurt am Main, 1974), 39.

fied view of human relations, but instead presents the secular-negative manifestation of real-life relations. And that's also true for Handke's individual perception, for introspection is also presented as a kind of negative epiphany, since it in fact consists of the radical strangeness of the seen, which then correlates to one's own sense of self-alienation. When Handke describes his journey as if it were an exploration of an alien world, this finds its correlation in the self-alienation that remains irreducibly opaque, but for which he thinks he has found its analogy. He describes the world of La Défense as if it were to him a foreign culture, and under which lies a peculiar fascination, because within it he discovers a materialization of his own alienation.

This ambivalence of the text, which constantly oscillates between the outer and inner view, between critique and affirmation, is perhaps most clear in the sense of the dislocation that

15.1 Peter Handke, *La Défense*; in Peter Handke, "Die Reise nach La Défense," in *Als das Wünschen noch geholfen hat* (Frankfurt am Main, 1974), 40.

underlies signs. Thus the text begins with a distinction between views on the ground and views above, between an indirect and a direct perception of Handke's surroundings. While out of reflex he looks for the "superiority of cut-off nature" on the ground and within that finds the residue of civilization and fragments of perception inherent to *signs* of the "monumental alienation of the expressions of human life" (Handke 31), he then looks up and realizes through this "settlement from another world" (Handke 32) that the world appears to consist entirely of signs, which are decipherable for him as a visitor: signs on the walls, signs for the banks and firms that have invested here, and not least of all a ritualization of the everyday, which appears to consist of the pure trafficking in signs. Handke observes a theatricalization of the manifestations of the citizens' lives. Their interaction is marked by "isolated ceremonies," and their everyday affairs reveal themselves as rituals

15.2 Peter Handke, *La Défense*; in Peter Handke, "Die Reise nach La Défense," in *Als das Wünschen noch geholfen hat* (Frankfurt am Main, 1974), 49.

"that perpetuate the illusion of being connected to the outside world" (Handke 32). Yet precisely this is what so fascinates the observer, such that he no longer knows how to distinguish between self-observation and being observed by others; for the observational distance is altered as the observer recognizes his own sense of alienation in this alienated world. It's not just the workings of the rituals of this "other world" that interest Handke — a world that really can be described as a "restricted area," because within it the "secrets of the technocracy" are open and undisguised — but rather their resonance, their correspondence to the observer himself: "The strangest thing of all was," according to Handke, "that I felt good inside. . . . It seemed to me as if my consciousness had finally found an external place that spoke to it on the inside" (Handke 35). The experimental nature of the journey into the near-at-hand aims also here at a discovery of an undisguised reality, at a strange view that opens a new perspective upon the supposedly familiar. Here, however, the undisguised reveals itself to be a surface of ordered signs and rituals, behind which there is nothing more to discover.

Peter Handke's travel account can be read as a programmatic text for his own work as well as for contemporary literature. While, most recently, he turned a reflection about signs into literature in his tetralogy *Slow Homecoming*, in which natural, cultural, and individual systems of signs are considered transposed on one another in complex ways, and juxtaposed to one another in new ways, we also find in contemporary German literature positions that aim not at a synthesis but rather a destruction of the social and mass media systems of signs that are so prevalent. Without question, one of the best known is that of Rolf Dieter Brinkmann. While in his early work he still held to the notion that one can reveal through the practice of photography an undisguised reality, he turns most recently in *Rom, Blicke* (*Rome, Glimpses*) to the work of destruction and, to use Theodor Adorno's words, "determinate negation." Brinkmann also presents his transit through mass media as a journey, which in collages, journals, and notes he takes up in his Cologne apartment, day in day out. "And so I traveled," he says in an epigraph for his posthumously published *Erkundungen für die Präzisierung des Gefühls für einen Aufstand* (*Investigations toward a Detailed Description of the Feeling of Revolt*), "with quiet eyes through each moment / I travel cool and undisguised through images & sentences / I see for the first time the actual horror of the present" (Brinkmann 6). The room of Brinkmann's miniature journey is no longer one through the space and time of a rarefied sanctuary or an archive full of objects that can be mistaken for life and history and can begin to speak on their own, but rather one overrun with images and texts of a world made stereotypical and standardized by mass media, one which thwarts reality and prevents an authentic life. For Handke, as well as for Brinkmann, the miniature journey asks less a question of cognition than one about the "pleasant day" and the "pleasant life." For Brinkmann, however, words and images have been placed before the objects themselves and thus have replaced them. The present has become a phantom that he searches for without ceasing, and which always disappears the moment you think you have it in hand. What remains is the journey through the present, even if it's decidedly one of destruction undertaken through images and language. Because behind the accursed images and words waits the wished-for life. For Handke, this leads later on after his tetralogy *Slow Homecoming*—and this is much more constructive than Brinkmann—to literature becoming life written out, and sometimes in an essay, nothing less than the worth of life depends on it. And thus it's no wonder that it's always about the journey, and not least of all the kind that covers only a few meters.

Travel Reading

Altenberg, Peter. "Ashantee." In Alternberg, *Wie ich es sehe*. Berlin, 1914. 295–332.

Augé, Marc. "Mémoire, image, oubli." In Marc Augé and Jean Mounicq, *Paris retraversé*. Paris, 1992, no page.

———. *Non-places*. Trans. John Howe. London and New York, 1995.

———. *La Traversée du Luxembourg: Paris, 29 juillet 1984; Ethno-Roman d'une journée française considérée sous l'angle des mœrs de la théorie et du bonheur*. Paris, 1985.

Bessis, Raphaël. *Dialogue avec Marc Augé autour d'une anthropologie de la mondialisation*. Paris, 2004.

Brinkmann, Rolf Dieter. *Erkundungen für die Präzisierung des Gefühls für einen Aufstand*. Reinbeck bei Hamburg, 1987.

Certeau, Michel de. *L'Invention du quotidien*. Paris, 1990 (vol. 1) and 1994 (vol. 2).

Handke, Peter. "Die offenen Geheimnisse der Technokratie." In Handke, *Als das Wünschen noch geholfen hat*. Frankfurt am Main, 1974. 31–38.

Kramer, Fritz. *Schriften zur Ethnologie*. Frankfurt am Main, 2005.

Lévi-Strauss, Claude. *Tristes Tropiques*. Trans. John Russell. New York, 1972.

Journeys into the World as Text

The seeking for my home . . . was my affliction. . . . Where is—my home? I ask and seek and have sought for it; I have not found it.

> Friedrich Nietzsche, *Thus Spoke Zarathustra*; quoted by Walter Benjamin in *The Arcades Project*, 20

No matter how no matter where. Time and grief and self so-called. Oh all to end.

> Beckett, 265

O. is sitting at his desk in front of the window.

> Simon, 178

There are restless travelers, such as Thorsten Becker, who traipse through the world and then suddenly come upon Xavier de Maistre's little travel book, and after reading it, all at once decide they must change their lives. In his, incidentally, both disparate and schematic book *Mitte* (*Middle*), which covers the time from December 1989 to September 1993, Becker not only sketches out stories parabolically while reporting on his travels through Germany, Greece, Algeria, Italy, Switzerland, Austria, France, Belgium, and the Netherlands—partially organized by the Goethe-Institut (which is simply referred to as "Goethe" throughout the text, thus like Rolf Dieter Brinkmann's essential text *Rom, Blicke* (*Rome, Glimpses*), harkening implicitly to Goethe's travels as a countermodel)—he also places in the middle of his book a completely new translation of de Maistre's room journey.

To be constantly traveling—that was, according to Becker, his everyday existence, "really the life that I imagined for myself. To be traveling, without having to pay to experience landscapes, panoramas, and a change of mood. Then to be expected by others at my destination. Really" (Becker 55). This "really" heralds a radical crisis that begins with observation, turning restlessness, helplessness, and homelessness into constants in his life. "My homelessness, my always needing to press further, my simultaneous tendency to always go too far, all that remains unchanged" (Becker 81).

Via Jochen Gerz's *Der Transsib.-Prospekt* from *documenta* 1977, which explicitly alludes to Xavier de Maistre and which we will encounter again in the next leg, Becker discovers that the middle of the book turns into a caesura, and in multiple ways. It's not just the doubling of the self, which is a central discovery of de Maistre in his book, but also the reevaluation of the journey already undertaken—regardless of whether it is a room journey—according to de Maistre's principles. "I had to live," says Becker, "thirty-three years to come upon a work while taking a detour that showed me that all the journeys I had made previously had turned into lost time" (Becker 200). He goes on, "Really, two hundred years after the completion of *Voyage autour de ma chambre* there can be no more modern or more comfortable method of travel, and thus we do not tarry and no longer pass a single day of ordinary life. De Maistre left the door of his room open behind him, and we step inside. We complete his journey, and through it we begin a new one of our own" (Becker 199). De Maistre's book is thus a lifesaver and a transformer of lives, since it also restores a place of refuge to the restless. It becomes a model that Becker not only translates but also updates in expanded chapters to appreciate the hopelessness of his undertaking: "The difference between the journey through one's room and all previously known types of travel is in the fact that no return is possible. Wherever a traveler travels to, he finds that, just when the journey would seem to be over, he is in the home to which he is able to return. This is not so on the journey through one's room. . . . My room looms up before me more foreign than the most foreign desert on the most distant planet: I am lost" (Becker 217). Everything that for de Maistre had served as orientation is now today useless: the mirror of morals, the meaning of images, reading and religion as well. Journeys such as room journeys lead to nothing. They lead only to the realm of pure existence itself.

In his book, Thorsten Becker touches on the expression of a philosophical worldview that, almost half a century before the change that his book focuses on, exiled human existence to a room. Julien Gracq, in his book on André Breton, accused the existentialists of turning the playful notion of a "journey around my room" into a deadly earnest "journey around my prison cell," thereby positing the locked-in nature of the human being as the *conditio humana*. Jean-Paul Sartre's *Huis clos* (*No Exit*) supposedly describes, in comparison, not the exception but the rule. The human being's room becomes a spatial abbreviation of his existence, and the room journey a symbol of his way of life. When one can no longer leave the room, which here becomes an emblem of subjective as well as intersubjective isolation, room travel is no longer possible — or at least only in entirely different ways.

Samuel Beckett explored this closed-off, almost immobile space from his earliest novels right up through his late prose pieces, such as "Stirrings Still," the last one published in his lifetime, making it both a point of departure and a culmination of the plot, if we can even speak of it as such. And it almost seems as if the room in "Stirrings Still" echoes the journeys taken by de Maistre, especially the nocturnal ones: "One night as he sat at his table head on hands he saw himself rise and go. One night or day. For when his own light went out he was not left in the dark. Light of a kind came then from the high window. Under it still the stool on which till he could or would no more he used to mount to see the sky. Why he did not crane out to see what lay beneath was perhaps because the window was not made to open or because he could or would not open it. Perhaps he knew only too well what lay beneath and did not wish to see it again. So he would simply stand there high above the earth and see through the clouded pane the cloudless sky. Its faint unchanging light unlike any light he could remember from the days and nights when day followed hard on night and night on day. This outer light then when his own went out became his only light till it in its turn went out and left him in the dark. Till it in its turn went out" (Beckett 259). A closed room, in which the view from the window provides neither a glimpse into the self nor a view of the world, and in which, as in de Maistre, the doubling and repetition enter in. Yet the discovery of the double brings no metaphysical insight, and repetition no pleasing memory. The double becomes a simulacrum of one's own existence, and the work of repetition only the repetition of the same thing over and over. The room doubles as his own skull, to which Beckett is finally reduced: neither subject nor object, neither matter nor consciousness, but rather a room that one cannot leave, and that can be explored only with effort. He is the beginning and end point of every psychic and physical movement, but also at the same time of each journey. Here time is turned into space; this, however, is transformed into the spatially described figures of the repetition. When Beckett turns the space of the room and that of the skull into a place for the repetition of the same thing, as well as the doubling and the observation of such, he thus also describes an existence that allows the room journey to become a symbol of existence.

What Beckett himself felt to be an end point was then transformed in the French literature of the mid-twentieth century into a new point of departure by which the space of the room was radically transformed. When we follow the development of French literature from Beckett (who as a resident of Paris is considered a part of French literature) to the *roman nouveau* through to the Tel Quel Group, we can observe first and foremost that numerous texts take off on the narrow confines of a room. From Claude Simon to Alain Robbe-Grillet, right through to Maurice Roche, Philippe Sollers, and Kamal Ibrahim, many literary texts concentrate primarily on the obsessive description of rooms. Thus in Robbe-Grillet the room nearly becomes a poetic phantasm, all his texts playing with motifs such as the voyeur, the labyrinth, the interlocking of rooms with changing views within them and from them, with repeated figures in the description, present and absent narrators, and even not least of all a radicalization of literary strategies of visualization. In *La Jalousie* (*Jealousy*), from which Robbe-Grillet's commentary is taken from a signed copy of the German first edition, the narrator, through detailed and multifaceted description, produces a scene in which he, without ever saying "I" once, is continually present as an absent figure within a narrative space. Through the minute description of single objects, this suggests a visual objectivity which, through the complex repetitive structure on the one hand, and on the other the affective interlacing of the narrator into the narration, results in a fragile construction.* The semantic ambivalence of "jalousie"† mirrors the oscillation between the

---

* "In a pinch one could say, in order to make fun of *La Jalousie*, that nothing really happens within it, that it's about people who each day drink the same aperitif on the terrace, Perrier with cognac. . . . Three people drink the aperitif and it is always the same scene, such that the good Emile Henriot even writes in his article for *Le Monde* that he has the impression of having found a bad copy of the book. . . . In his eyes it always seems to be the same scene which plays out with some variations, but without any intrigue ever developing. In reality it develops, but he doesn't notice that it does" (Robbe-Grillet 88).

† *Translator's note*: Besides meaning "jealousy," a "jalousie" is also what we know as a Venetian blind.

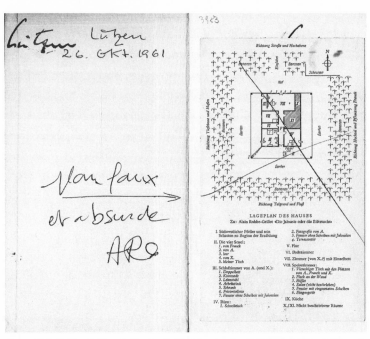

16.0 Alain Robbe-Grillet, dedication in *Die Jalousie oder die Eifersucht* (Munich, 1959). Author's collection.

inner and the outer view, between self-perception and perception by others, between inner and outer space, between the space of the room and that of the self that nearly engenders the space of the story from the start.

Nearly twenty decades later, literature is understood as a room journey. "Alone in a room a person sees, dreams, and writes," it says on the jacket copy of Philippe Sollers's *The Park*. That can be said of many novels and stories. And when the narrator writes, "How many voyages . . . without leaving his chair" (Sollers 32), this also speaks to the prose of his time.

And now one example among many: in Claude Simon's novel *The Battle of Pharsalus*, there's a subtle blending together of observations, fragments of memory, historical dates, and reflections, as well as layers of time, etc. — things such as battles from the Roman civil war and the Second World War, but also the street battles in Paris in 1968, being alluded to throughout — whose source is often taken from single objects within the narrator's field of vision. On a pack of Gauloises, a familiar helmet with wings is depicted: just such a pack lies on the desk of the narrator who then transforms it into a flying helmet, then into wings, then a helmet that serves to protect one from being wounded in an all-out battle, and so on. The same thing happens with other objects that he finds on his desk or very close by. Simon also draws such a writing scene. One sees a desk next to an open window.

In Simon's *The Battle of Pharsalus*, however, this description of a room with a view is doubled in complicated ways when the first sentence of the text is repeated at the end, but this time with the point of view turned around. While at the start of the novel the view rises from a street café upward to a window, the perspective is turned around at the end. When the view of the empty piece of paper on his desk occurs and a writing scene is imagined in which it would seem most likely to see what we have just read, the empty page thus becomes an unfathomable space of narration. Both cases have to do with observers observed, which implicates the reader in this complex game, which in French literature since André Gide is known as *mise en abyme*.

"Both the journey and the battle take place in the narrator's room on his desk" (Becker 85). The room is the beginning and end point of the description. It is a reduced and expanded space at once. Now the fact that a man sits in a room and writes is considered the normal condition in which literature is produced — regardless of exceptions such as literature produced in cafés. Yet even with authors like Marcel Proust, whose room indeed took on nearly mythic qualities, the space used for writing is not the subject but rather the opposite: now the room is purely the place of language itself. One must no longer leave the room to describe the world, for it is already prepared to be written, and only able to be grasped in the form of language and writing. While we find throughout Claude Simon's work a continual stream of historical references, autobiographical fragments, recollections, countless allusions to the applied arts and literature, and not least of all photography, in the texts of the Tel Quel Group, at the latest, a self-referential system takes shape in which the act of writing explores the world of language, which also purports to be the world itself. In this era of the textualization of the world, in which we often encounter the idea that the world cannot be grasped just through language, but rather that language is an impenetrable component of human existence, literature turns into the production of a textual space that claims to be a space in the world. This is even true of the, in every sense, debauched sexual fantasies in Kamal Ibrahim's *La voyage de cent mètres* (*The Journey of a Hundred Meters*), which are generated through a virtual language machine into which sexually coded words are fed, and which then spits out verbal associations — in some ways the spitting-out and feeding-in also take on a sexual feel, thereby turning the language machine into a fantasy.

Even when the inherent laws of language are explored and the narrator (as well as the reader) becomes lost in the countless filiations found in wordplay and the endlessly winding labyrinth of language, in which, if we read Michel Foucault as literature, also the minotaur and other classical figures enjoy a happy revival, at no point is describable reality forsaken; rather, it is primarily formulated through the verbal. The descriptions of it are not made weary by the passage of words, even if it is a thousand words and behind a thousand sentences no world exists.

We also find in the literature of this period a playful form of room journey. Ilse Kilic and Fritz Widhalm founded a journal called *Das fröhliche Wohnzimmer* (*The Cheery Home*) devoted to reflections on language, and in the process they produced a number of funny and original texts. In conjunction with its twentieth

16.1 Claude Simon, *Study in Salses*; in Irene Albers, *Photographische Momente bei Claude Simon* (Würzburg, 2002), 156.

anniversary, there appeared in 2004 a *Fest- und Forschschrift* for which Xavier de Maistre's room journey and Jules Verne's Phileas Fogg were clearly the models. Jana Brenessel and i.g. Naz, the fictional protagonists of this narrative exploration, are sent on an eighty-day journey through the eight rooms of the cheery home. Armed with a map, which could have been taken from Robert Louis Stevenson's *Treasure Island* or Edgar Allan Poe's "The Gold Bug," they undertake an actual research expedition that includes camping in tents at the spot where they arrive. Texts, images, and songs are linked to one another and a symbolic space is explored which is meant to yield experiences. Examples are taken from Oulipo, or more precisely the *Ouvroir de littérature potentielle* (*Workshop of Potential Literature*), and the "Wiener Gruppe." The Oulipean Georges Perec in particular took up the theme of the room and the movement of the travel narrative in some of his own texts, not least of all in his wonderful book *Life: A User's Manual*, in which he heads out from a Paris apartment building whose façade has been removed and that is presented as open to the reader's inspection. This kind of viewing of the interior of a building can already be found in nineteenth-century engravings and today particularly in children's books. Perec creates out of this an elaborate experiment, through which he not only follows diverse *contraintes*, including self-imposed rules (such as having in each chapter a quote from Herman Melville and Vladimir Nabokov, or bringing in allusions to John Coltrane), but also is able to let the reader put the text together like a puzzle, whose totality leads to yet another image formed. Hence, the closed space of the room is turned into the open space of reading.

In the 1940s, Jorge Luis Borges had in fact already tried to describe the world as a dense web of texts that in a fantastic manner contained all of reality. In the famous story "The Aleph," de Maistre functions as a model for this appropriation of world literature—first in the form of the renunciation of travel, then through

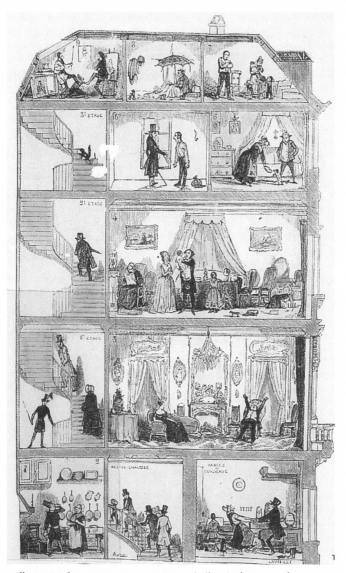

16.2 Illustration from Georges Perec, *La Vie mode d'emploi* (Paris, 1978).

explicit reference: "He observed," says Carlos Argentino Daneris, the likewise enigmatic and fascinating counterpart to the narrator, who carries Borges's own name, "that for a man so equipped, the act of traveling was supererogatory; this twentieth century of ours had upended the fable of Muhammad and the mountain—mountains nowadays did in fact come to the modern Muhammad" (Borges 276). And de Maistre's story functions for him as a parallel, indeed as the logical consequence of the mythical Aleph, in which the entire world converges. The composition is titled "The Earth" and concerns itself with nothing more, although also nothing less than the entire planet—without leaving the room in the process—since, as it says: "For the *voyage* that I narrate is . . . *autour de ma chambre*" (Borges 276). The same goes for the mythical Aleph, "one of the points in space that contain all points" (Borges 280). All that is needed is to descend into the cellar in order to look up at the nineteen sets of stairs to the corresponding floors and thus see the "inconceivable universe" (Borges 284) in a single point—and yet have to forget it again. That is the beginning and also the end of literature.

Travel Reading

Becker, Claudia. *Zimmer-Kopf-Welten: Zur Motivgeschichte des Intérieurs im 19. und 20. Jahrhundert*. Munich, 1990. 82–131.

Becker, Thorsten. *Mitte*. Berlin, 1994.

Beckett, Samuel. "Stirrings Still." In *The Complete Short Prose 1929–1989*. Ed. S. E. Gontarski. Grove, 1995. 259–65.

Borges, Jorge Luis. "The Aleph." In *Collected Fictions*. Trans. Andrew Hurley. New York, 1998. 274–88.

Foucault, Michel. *Schriften zur Literatur*. Frankfurt am Main, 1993.

Gracq, Julien. *André Breton: Quelques aspects de l'écrivain*. Paris, 1948.

Ibrahim, Kamal. *Le Voyage de cent mètres*. With a foreword, "Grille pour un parcours imaginaire," by Joyce Mansour. Paris, 1979.

Kilic, Ilse, and Fritz Widhalm. *Reise in 80 Tagen durch das Wohnzimmer: Eine Fest- und Forschschrift*. Vienna, 2004.

Perec, Georges. *Life: A User's Manual*. Trans. David Bellos. Boston, 1987.

Robbe-Grillet, Alain. *La Jalousie*. Paris, 1957 (German edition, *Die Jalousie oder die Eifersucht*. Munich, 1959).

———. *Dans le labyrinthe*. Paris, 1959.

———. *Préface à une d'écrivain*. Paris, 2005.

Roche, Maurice. *Compact*. Paris, 1966 (German edition, *Kompakt*. Köln, 1972).

Schütte, Wolfram. *Das Fernste im Nächsten* (review of German translation of de Maistre's book from June 1, 2006). http://www.titel -magazin.de/modules.php?op=modload&name=News&file =article&sid=4665.

Simon, Claude. *The Battle of Pharsalus*. Trans. Richard Howard. New York, 1971.

Sollers, Philippe. *The Park*. Trans. A. M. Sheridan Smith. Red Dust, 1981.

The Journey into Oneself

Rather than outward or at anything outside, I prefer to direct
my gaze in a self-critical manner toward my inner life, or at my
inner world. There the white flecks of the unknown can still
be surmised, and only there is it possible to step into the new
country of a mysterious *terra incognita*.

    Timm Ulrichs

Nature knows no limits.

    Leibniz, quoted in von Renard 106

In the science-fiction novel *Un Homme chez les microbes* (*A Man
among Microbes*) by the now unknown French author Maurice Renard, we find a long excerpt from a letter written by Leibniz to
Bernoulli: "What I cannot help but notice, though it doesn't disturb me, is that there are animals in the universe that are larger
than our own, just as ours are larger than other animalcules (mi-
croscopic animals) one can only see with the aid of a microscope,
since nature knows no limits. To the contrary, there can and there
must exist in the smallest speck of dust, in the tiniest atom, entire
worlds that are no less beautiful and multifaceted than our own."
Present within this is a type of complementary order of both the
near and the far, whereby the space of the world expands in the
same way that any beloved object also contains an infinite realm

within it. This is what escapes our senses, according to Renard, whether it is the large or the small, the stars or the microbes. The universe opens out in both directions. And we can explore it — in this case, in the guise of the research scientist Fléchambeau, who is shrunk to the size of an atom and deep within the heart of things discovers a new world called "Ourrh" populated by "Micromégas." The inhabitants have Greek names like Agathos, Kakos, or Kalos, as well as an advanced culture as technologically sophisticated as our own, and which has at its command something called "pom-pon" that allows pure ideas and feelings to be transmitted from one individual to another without having to make use of any me-dium for such transmissions. Ourrh is in part a system of stars that resembles the Earth's solar system, which is often alluded to. Maeterlinck (Renard 142ff.) and Pascal (Renard 155ff.) are quoted, and there are also museums and an extremely civilized society that is threatened only by the "Hons," fungi that spread quickly and take over the surface of the planet. They can be controlled only by general sterilization, and as a result this mandarin people has become sterile, though because of their immortality this is not all that problematic. Then the inevitable occurs: the fungi begin to spread anew, but the shrunken scientist can save his civiliza-tion and exterminate the fungi. Thus is founded a type of imagi-nary and miniaturized exploration of the world that would go on to have many different manifestations, and which would even ap-pear again as a "real" miniature journey — almost literally.

The world is endless — it gets ever bigger. Especially if we con-sider the year 1966 and the adventure of the spaceship *Proteus*, whose crew journeys for some hours while discovering new worlds, new life, and new realms. Just a few centimeters below the surface of the skin, *Proteus* passes through galaxies never before seen by man. Such is the amazing journey in a submarine through a human body that Richard Fleischer captured in images in his film *Fantastic Voyage*, which today seems to us like an illustra-

17.0 Richard Fleischer, *Fantastic Voyage*; film still.

tion of the psychedelic visions of the 1960s: boiling oceans of pink bubbles, excreting walls full of guck, jellyfish-like creatures that drift through tunnels that have a cell-like consistency. Fleischer, who had already filmed Jules Verne's *20,000 Leagues under the Sea*, made use of an outline from Isaac Asimov that only later appeared as a book. The plot is as absurd as it is simple. During the Cold War, a scientist who has developed a means of shrinking bodies is shot as he is being secretly smuggled across the border. To get rid of a blood clot in his head, his method is employed, and the shrunken submarine *Proteus* is injected into his body. Predictably, there is a traitor onboard who just as predictably is thwarted so that he cannot prevent the others from saving the scientist's life. Naturally, this also involves them risking their own lives, since the time that they can remain shrunk is limited, and the path through the bloodstream is long and winding. At the end, they are rescued through the eye and the scientist is saved; otherwise his body would have exploded.

This film was the inspiration for a painting by Salvador Dali and won an Oscar for best special effects. The plot was also the inspiration for a very successful cartoon series whose seventeen thirty-minute episodes were broadcast on ABC between 1968 and 1970, and last but not least it was also the target of Joe Dante's slapstick remake, *Innerspace*. The theme of being shrunk also appears in numerous films, the best known of which is Jack Arnold's B-movie cult classic, *The Incredible Shrinking Man*. Beyond such memorable sentences as "The philosophers of the Middle Ages were right. Man is the center of the universe. In the middle of eternity we stand between inner and outer space. And both are limitless," or the one used to describe blood plasma as being "just like seawater, an ocean of life stretching one hundred thousand miles from one end to another," Fleischer's film fits the notion of traveling in place explored here only to the extent that it later inspired an artistic event which depicted an actual journey through the body as a visual journey. This refers to Timm Ulrich's *Durchsicht: durchs Ich; Eine endoskopische Reise* (*The View Through: Through Me; An Endoscopic Journey*). In his video *Reise zum Mittelpunkt des Ichs* (*Journey to the Middle of Myself*) (1995/97), Ulrich had already analyzed his body layer by layer with an MRI and thus commenced a peculiar type of journey that alludes to Jules Verne's novel *Journey to the Center of the Earth* when he renders himself as a series of images on the way to the middle of his skull. Ulrich thus created the artistic version of what for some time has been made accessible to natural scientists on the Internet through the Visible Human Project. There, both a male and a female body are dissected into millimeter-size axial segments, which are then photographed and digitalized. On the Internet, we can now take a visual journey through the human body. And if you don't want to go on the Internet, you can buy Alexander Tsiaras's book *Body Voyage*, which also comes with a CD. The title

17.1 Richard Fleischer, *Fantastic Voyage*; film still.

is self-explanatory, for it's an exploration of space, in fact a journey through the body as space—even if it can only be depicted through individual shots. And on the Internet, we can also book a special guided tour without having to pay a cent: A Guided Tour of the Visible Human, on which we are led through the body from head to toe in 135 segments.

"Space exploration doesn't require traveling great distances in order to ramble about the macrocosm. What the inner world, the microcosm, contains is what we experience instead by researching the inner realm, by entering the subterranean subcutaneous realm of our own bodily nature, that which lies in the dark chamber of our head, in the body's frame, which always remains perpetually in darkness, and onto which so little of the light of understanding has been shed. Curious to discover unforeseeable sights and un-imagined experiences in my own body, I have frequently set off

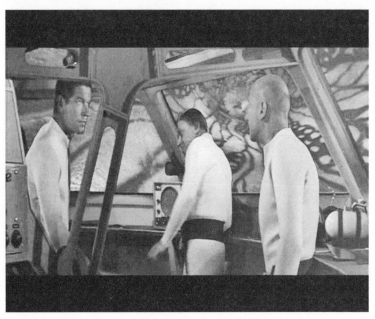

17.2 Richard Fleischer, *Fantastic Voyage*; film still.

on a journey into myself, to descend into the subsurface and pit of myself, or my Self. The head that has been x-rayed and thus peeled open and minimized looks like a heavenly body, which at the same time, as if on a time journey, seems to reveal a phylogenetic retrogression—from humans to apes to fish—until finally, like a small, lost, twinkling star that has drifted off into the blackness of the All or the Nothing, its nucleus appears with a last flash from its core." So Timm Ulrichs describes his first exploration, which later, in an explicit allusion to Fleischer's film, had a second manifestation. Like Jochen Gerz's *Der Transsib.-Prospekt*, which we'll look at on the next leg of our journey, Ullrichs's work was shown at the *documenta 6*, the biannual art show held in Kassen. At that time, there did not yet exist the technical means which years later Ulrichs employed to realize his long-expressed intention by swallowing

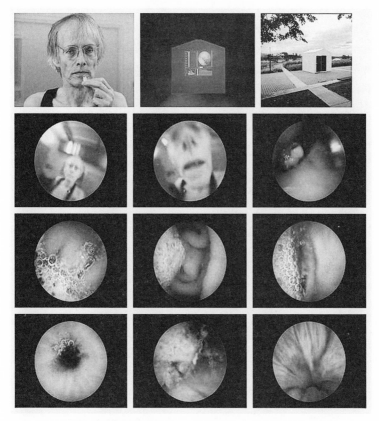

17.3 Timm Ulrichs, *The View Through: Through Me; An Endoscopic Journey*; in Cornelia Gockel. "Reise zum Ich. Der Blick in das Innere des Körpers in der Kunst nach 1960," *Innovation* 19, no. 3 (2008): 50.

a miniature camera that then broadcast endoscopic images of his physique on a screen. "This allows images to surface that no travel prospectus has ever been able to offer, nor any Baedeker can elucidate. The deeper we press into ourselves, the more we sink into our own physique and psyche, until we are struck by how inscrutable, unfathomable, uncanny, and strange we are, until we recognize what we are: foreign bodies."

Travel Reading

Arnold, Jack. *The Incredible Shrinking Man.* 81 min. USA, 1957.

Asimov, Isaac. *Fantastic Voyage.* Boston, 1966.

Fleischer, Richard, director. *Fantastic Voyage.* 101 min. USA, 1966.

Guided Tour of the Visible Human. http://www.madsci.org/~lynn/VH/tour.html.

Renard, Maurice. *Un homme chez les microbes.* Paris, 1956 (first edition, Paris, 1920).

Tsiaras, Alexander. *Body Voyage: Eine 3D-Reise durch die Körper-welten.* Heidelberg, Munich, 1998.

Ulrichs, Timm. *Durchsicht: Durchs Ich; Eine endoskopische Reise.* http://www.kunstprojekt-goetzen.de/56.0.html.

EIGHTEENTH LEG

Crossing-Crisscrossing

I dreamt that I took the entire building and constructed it
elsewhere. There lived my father and my mother, the older
family members lying dead in the cellar, the brothers living
above, while all around lived women and men who had no
idea what to do. Somewhere in a corner sat a big woman who
kept having children and tossing them into the world. I was
somewhere inside and kept on digging.

Schneider, *Kunsthalle Bern*, 55

Now I have the feeling that the window is looking at me.

Schneider, *Kunsthalle Bern*, 55

The French artists group Ici-Même (Here in This Place), whose
name implies its program, began on February 15, 2002, a journey
by foot across the populated areas of Grenoble. One self-imposed
undertaking of this event, which was linked with three others that
formulated new tasks for specific places in the city, was for one
of the travelers to spend the night with a resident whom he had
not previously known. Out of this event a book was produced that
was like a dictionary with entries from A to Z, which the par-
ticipants wrote together. Clearly relying on the rhizomatic philosophy of Gilles Deleuze, the book oscillates between theoretical
reflections, diary entries, and the documentation of the events in
image and text. There we find in the entry for "Tuesday, the 16th of

18.0, 18.1 Ici-Même, cover of *Les Paysages étaient extraordinaires* (Grenoble, 2004).

Cette conversation
fait-elle partie
du spectacle ?

Qui avez-vous vu ?

Savez-vous
depuis combien de temps
vous êtes là ?

Que faites-vous ce soir ?

Sommes-nous en train
de nous rencontrer ?

Est-ce que vous faites
partie du public ?

Pouvez-vous encore
voir la beauté
des montagnes ?

Avez-vous dormi tranquille ?

April, 2002, 4 p.m., while under way" the following information: "Dedicated to a book by X. de Maistre titled *Voyage autour de ma chambre*" (Ici-Même, no page). It's thus obviously not just about the traveler traveling into the near-at-hand in order to experience it and explore the here-and-now, but also about bringing a message to the traveled, if such a neologism is allowed, along the way: Follow the path on your own and explore the world around you. Cross the near-at-hand and thwart its transformation into a stereotypical dead space. The journey through the near-at-hand consists of and has a political function.

One such exploration of the cityscape can also take on disproportionately foreboding aspects. Jeff Chapman published under the pseudonym Ninjalicious a zine called *Infiltration*, founded a website with the same name, and published shortly before his death a *Guide to the Art of Urban Exploration*. As a genuine activist in the exploration of the urban underground, for him it's about the hidden sides of the city: tunnels and hospitals, sewers and cellars, fountains and subway shafts, abandoned buildings and military grounds, factory ruins and dead zones of the city—almost all no-go areas whose attraction lies precisely in the sign that says Entry Forbidden and whose space begins only behind the same.

Yet the notion of overcoming the sense of the indifference of the everyday through the mindset of the traveler can also be found in numerous less dangerous (and also less politically motivated) variations in contemporary art, as well as in popular culture. Many blogs and postings on the Internet sites Flickr, YouTube, or other such sites (a few of them set up as travel reading to take along) show room journeys and invite the visitor on a visual walk through their room. This is less voyeuristic than it sounds and more boring than perhaps one would reckon. Because what is there really to discover inside the room of a stranger when he is not home and the objects stand there alien and mute? Therefore, some room travelers have foregone the usual wide-angled, 360-degree shot (the room tour that often passes over the mirror in which the occupant then captures his own image) and instead estranged the objects by manipulating them through close-ups or extreme enlarging. And among such room journeys can be found one as enjoyable as Caroline Mollie's — so the room-traveling photographer is called who posted the fruits of her travels on the website Dailymotion — who apparently, without knowing ahead of time, carried Xavier de Maistre's project into the digital age: "For three years I photographed the construction of the tram from my window at the corner of Avenue Borriglione and Xavier-de-Maistre Street. What's funny is that the latter is what is described in his work *Voyage autour de ma chambre*" (http://www.dailymotion.com/carolinemollie).

Also in the predictable field of travel guides, we find some titles that are about another kind of journey, whose readers have not picked up their brochures from the travel agency. Along with travel guides for countries that don't exist, namely Molwanîen, San Sombrero, and Phaic Tan,* is one from the legendary travel series

---

* And for the touring of which Amazon.de offers the following: "Dream Destination Molwanîen. You have to go there. But you never can. For Molwanîen does not actually exist. But the first comprehensive guide to it does. And there one can find an entire country — complete with a language, history, restaurant tips, and garment sizes. This brilliant idea traveled around the world and became a best seller from Australia to Italy, for Molwanîen is everywhere. Our world has grown small: half a day's journey takes one halfway across the world, chock-full tourist flights land in the far corners of the Earth, nor is the smallest falafel stand in Damascus any longer a secret. Where, then, shall the restless human spirit of discovery travel to? Perhaps to a place within our imagination, perhaps to that place which tourists were long forbidden to enter, that legendary gem of Eastern Europe: Molwanîen. A friendly country in which already at breakfast a glass of 'Zeerstum' is served, the traditional garlic brandy, but which one should never imbibe. A place of pilgrimage for ornithologists in search of the rare Molwanîsh thrush, which every autumn in impressive formations flies off to its winter quarters 2.5 kilometers away, during which thousands become confused and die of exhaustion. It's also an oasis for lovers of pristine nature that can be found within Molwanîen's 'Great Plains,' a landscape that because of its incomparable wasteland and boredom was declared a world cultural heritage site by UNESCO. So, don't you want to go? Well, you cannot go, but you'll tell your friends about it anyway."

Lonely Planet that covers experimental journeys. The "Workshop of Potential Literature" (*Oulipo*) is now *Latourex*, the "LAboratoire de TOURisme EXpérimental," in other words the Laboratory for Experimental Tourism. This guide, written by two founders of Lonely Planet (and also the homepage of this singular institute of tourism), lists a good forty different forms of experimental travel, only a few of which can be listed here:

AIRPORT TRAVEL: Spend forty-eight hours in an airport without getting on a plane. Enjoy the comfortable lounges, the different washing facilities, the shops, and the various eateries. Watch people skip through to the departure lounge and let your eyes glaze over as you peruse the ever-changing departures board. (This is familiar — although without the option of going home — from the Tom Hanks film *The Terminal*.)

EXPEDITON TO K2: Explore the area on a town plan or map that occupies the square marked K2. Take full advantage of all cultural attractions, gastronomic delights, and watering holes in that area.

A–Z TRAVEL: Choose a town to visit from A to Z. Find the first road beginning with A and the last beginning with Z, and draw a line between the two. Walk the length of this line and discover the city alphabetically.

COUNTERTRAVEL: Travel with a camera, but don't take pictures of the famous landmarks and tourist attractions. Stand with your back to the site and snap that view instead.

LITERARY TRAVEL: Take a literary tour of the world without leaving your sitting room. Start with an author from your country, and then read a book by someone from a neighboring country. Continue until you make your route around the globe.

TRAVEL PURSUIT: Follow some friends when they go on holiday and don't let them out of your sight. Take lots of photos of them using a telephoto lens. On their return home, welcome them with a slideshow of their vacation. (Sophie Calle made this kind of journey into an art form, and Christopher Nolan made a film called *Following* that had to do with the fascinating and unforeseeable consequences of such an undertaking.)

*　*　*

Along with the *Voyage autour de ma chambre*, which above all serves as a follow-up to the journey already taken, we also find a surreal journey in which place-names are combined with one another to form an art sentence (these can be made up of toponyms such as Orange/Buffalo/Aurora or Caribou/Almond/Andes—as well as street names . . .) and which are then visited. Indeed, even André Breton *himself* reports from the heyday of surrealism on the peculiar journey taken to Blois, "a town we had picked at random on the map. It was agreed that we would head off haphazardly on foot, conversing all the while, and that our only planned detours would be for eating and sleeping. In actual practice, the project turned out to be quite peculiar, and even fraught with danger. The trip, which was scheduled to last for about ten days, but which we finally cut short, immediately took an initiatory turn. The absence of any goal soon removed us from reality, gave rise beneath our feet to increasingly numerous and disturbing phantoms. We easily fell prey to irritation, and there was even a violent episode between Aragon and Vitrac. All things considered, the exploration was hardly disappointing, no matter how narrow its range, because it probed the boundaries between waking life and dream life. So it fell wholly within the scope of our concerns at that time" (Breton 59–60).

Also in the realm of the applied arts, we find countless works that take up the motif of travel. To name just a couple of examples, there is Rémy Markowitsch, who in his installations combines images and texts of Claude Lévi-Strauss with numerous other travel accounts and photos into complex constellations of their own; or Lisl Ponger, whose journeys through Vienna turn into a journey through different continents. The journey with and through art becomes the development of a new realm of experience and counters the expectations, as well as the habits, of the viewer.

Already a good thirty years ago, Jochen Gerz presented at *documenta 6* in 1977 his installation *Der Transsib.-Prospekt*, which can be found today in the Wiesbaden Museum. The title itself plays with one of those mythic journeys that still draws hundreds of travelers, as well as containing the ambivalence of the idea of a "Prospekt" or "brochure" as a starting point for a particular journey. Just like a printed brochure, it lists tourist sights all along the travel route, as in fact happens for those who take the journey today. In playing off of a "prospect" as a "view," Gerz plays with not only time and space but also the view from the train window, the description of which in the nineteenth century was tied to the change in perception that came with the modern. However, when one views the installation, it's no longer possible to determine whether Gerz really took this journey, or whether he is just playing with the viewer's imagination. All one sees is sixteen roof slates and behind them sixteen arranged chairs.

This journey, or rather the installation, had a clear experimental purpose: Gerz undertook a sixteen-day and sixteen-night journey with the Trans-Siberian Railway, which he passed, à la Raymond Roussel, in a half-darkened train compartment with closed and covered windowpanes. During this trip he brought along sixteen slates, one for each day, on which he placed his naked feet. All other evidence of the journey was destroyed. All that was left was the impression of his feet on the slates — or at least what one takes to be this. These slates then became a part of the installation. In the sketches for this project, Gerz lists an extensive array of travel literature, particularly room journeys such as de Maistre's, but also lesser-known texts, such as Alois Schreiber's *Reise meines Vetters auf seinem Zimmer* (*My Cousin's Travels in His Room*). An-

18.2 Jochen Gerz, *Der Transsib.-Prospekt*, Kassel, 1977; in Jochen Gerz, *Get Out of My Lies: 18 Installationen der siebziger Jahre* (Wiesbaden, 1997), 84.

other room traveler, Thorsten Becker, also includes Gerz in his book *Mitte* (*Middle*).

This peculiar ambivalence between real and imagined journeys also appears in press coverage. While in 1977 *Der Spiegel* still reported anecdotally that during the journey Gerz wrote nearly incessantly, and that the conductors called him "Pushkin," twenty-three years later no one seems to recall this. Now the *Berliner Zeitung* writes: "Asked if he ever really made this journey, he answers, 'Every journey happens inside one's head.'" This irritating oscillation is in fact a part of the overall concept. Gerz's work develops a theoretical model of art based on memory that is focused not on depiction but rather the viewer and the process of memory in order to reflect on how it actively works and its necessary actualization. Many of his works, which juxtapose the Shoah and the Nazi past, seek in their own way to elicit a train of thought that lasts longer than a shocking encounter.

The French photographer Jean-Paul Lubliner no longer traveled far away, but instead stayed constantly near a Paris tourist attraction: the Eiffel Tower. Here as well the artistic project follows a strict experimental concept. He moves only within a certain radius in which he can walk only two hundred meters in any direction. Each day he sends *Le Monde* two pictures, only one of which is published. And the time frame (perhaps luckily for him) is limited: the experiment lasts exactly one year and ends with the close of the millennium. "At the beginning it was still a game, then it became a drug, at times a trap. A picture per day was the rhythm. His gaze sharpens, becoming ever more attentive, yet also more free. He moves with the world around him, in contact with it, watching the sky, the birds, the people around him, those from the neighborhood, but also the tourists and the demonstrators on the Trocadéro. The radius in which he moves is limited: two-hundred meters left, two-hundred meters right. And yet each day he finds that some kind of encounter is buried within it. Each day is a surprise" (Lubliner, no page). At the close of this process, there appears a book with some of Lubliner's pictures presented in chronological order, as well as texts from various international journalists, rights activists, writers, and politicians (such as the ineluctable Jack Lang), all of whom try to formulate their wishes for the new millennium. These function as the literary-political pendant to the photos, while the clock that is running down appears to offer a peculiar message: "The clock for the year 2000 presents symbols like the oracle of Delphi" (Lubliner, no page).

We can take matters even further and set ourselves down on a flying carpet, or simply take one along. While the Austrian artist Monika Pichler works on silk screens that look like carpets, Pascal Tarabay and Catalina Tobon designed "Homes," portable "carpet houses," which can be folded up and carried away in order to always have our house with us (Simon 179). Pichler's works take up, as we have already seen on the Second Leg, the motif of the traveling "Frauenzimmer" of the nineteenth century, though they

18.3 Jean-Paul Lubliner, *Eiffel Tower*; in Jean-Paul Lubliner, *Tour Eiffel: Un Voyage immobile* (Paris, 2000), no page.

also play with the idea of the carpet as a filigreed structure, such that occasionally we see hidden maps or earthly conceptions of the Garden of Eden. With Pichler's work, the viewer perceives upon closer inspection that the supposedly idyllic motif displayed on the carpet also has images of oil-drenched birds or war scenes woven in, or even carries the title "Carpet Bombing" (Rathenböck).

18.4 Jean-Paul Lubliner, *Eiffel Tower*; in Jean-Paul Lubliner, *Tour Eiffel: Un Voyage immobile* (Paris, 2000), no page.

Or we can, as did Gregor Schneider with his captivating and legendary work *Totes Haus u r* (*Dead House u r*),[†] which was awarded

[†] Schneider differentiates between the original house and the installation at another location. Once removed, it becomes a dead house. "When Schneider takes away sections of the house and from them displays replicas, these components are no longer alive for him. They are no longer constituent parts of the organism, they are dead" (Birnbaum 80).

18.5 Gregor Schneider, *Haus u r*; in Jörg und Ralf Raimo Jung, *Gregor Schneider: Zuflucht oder Kerker* (Germany, 2001). 43 min. DVD booklet (absolut MEDIEN, 2008), 4.

the Golden Lion of the 2001 Venice Biennale, deconstruct a house over the course of a year until there is no longer any part that can be taken away without it collapsing. The house that Schneider had constructed in the German pavilion in Venice combined various rooms that in part came from the original *Haus u r*, which takes its name from **U**nterheydener Strasse 12 in **R**heydt, or stemmed from other works constructed for exhibitions, including some put together for the Biennale. During the Biennale, one could only explore this house and be subjected to a unique experience that Schneider imagined for his *Haus u r*. Over the course of many years, he had completely remodeled the inside of the house, such

Ich kann nie vorher wissen, wer zu welchem Zeitpunkt welche Tür öffnet.
Manchmal habe ich das Gefühl, dass plötzlich Personen auftauchen.
Ich erwarte jemanden, eine Türklinke fällt hinunter, und ich glaube, der Besuch sei schon da.
Es kann ein Sog entstehen, ein leichtes Dröhnen.
Vielleicht funktioniert der hinterste Raum wie ein Resonanzkörper.

18.6 Gregor Schneider, *Haus u r*. In Jörg und Ralf Raimo Jung, *Gregor Schneider: Zuflucht oder Kerker* (Germany, 2001). 43 min. DVD booklet (absolut MEDIEN, 2008), 4.

that the original order of the rooms was no longer recognizable. A house within a house. A room within a room. A wall before a wall. "Gregor Schneider . . . built, in old-fashioned terms, a house of his soul" (Kittelmann 16) and presented a "lived space" (Kittelmann 18) which also didn't fail to have an impact on the visitor. On YouTube we can find the documentation of a visit to *Haus u r* which, when looked at while nothing more than a viewer within the comfort of our own four walls, makes an impact.

Yet what can really be seen and experienced within this house? First of all, nothing less than a complex nesting of rooms, walls, and carpets, or, as Schneider's interviewer in an extensive and illuminating conversation summed up the work: "A wall before a wall, a wall before a wall, a wall behind a wall, a hallway in a room, a room within a room, a hallway in a room, a wall before a wall,

Ich habe nur erzählt, was ich zu der Zeit auch gemacht habe.
Ich habe nicht gelogen. Ich habe erzählt, dass ich Räume baue, die ich nicht als Raum im
Raum, Raum um Raum wahrnehme, dass plötzlich eine Wand da ist, die dann wieder weg
ist, dass ich auf eine Wand schaue und mich diese Unebenheiten interessieren,
das kleinste Loch, die kleinste Erhöhung.
Auf Grund dessen bin ich nicht zur Bundeswehr gekommen.

18.7   Gregor Schneider, *Haus u r*; In Jörg und Ralf Raimo Jung, *Gregor Schneider: Zuflucht oder Kerker* (Germany, 2001). 43 min. DVD booklet (absolut MEDIEN, 2008), 4.

blue flecks of paper in a wall, a room within a room, a room within a room, red brick behind a room, lead pipes around a room, lead pipes in the floor, light within a room, a wall before a wall, a shape within a wall, a cube within a wall, black brick within a wall, ceilings in motion beneath ceilings, a hallway in a room, a wall before a wall" (Schneider, *Kunsthalle Bern*, 21). This sounds banal, and yet it represents the complete transformation of a house of which nothing old is left and whose unique transformation should be able to be observed by the stranger traveling through and which, as impressed visitors to Venice and Rheydt report enthusiastically, in fact occurs. Each visitor should, according to Schneider, go through the house only once in order to explore it only once.

For Schneider, it's about the presentation of the impact that space has on us, which is barely measurable, but indeed can be experienced in the play of certainty and uncertainty, habit and change, conscious and unconscious perception, intimacy and discomfort. What is the effect of a space when altered? How about when I allow it, such as what happened in *Haus u r*, to be imperceptibly turned on its axis, such that the exit sometimes ends up being different and perhaps even leads into different rooms than before? Or when the light that presses through the window is artificial (but which is so finely installed that it doesn't feel so), and the visitor later leaves the house expecting it to be dark, but finds that the sun is still shining? Or when the rooms are laid up against one another, layer for layer and wall after wall like an onion, and rooms in between open up that we can step into, sometimes with only a notion of a further room, which bears witness to a seemingly hidden space that indeed strongly changes our perception of the space we are standing in? Or when the doors have no handles and the rooms no exits? Or when a cellar is turned into a hole filled with water? Or when I, to get to another room, have to crawl through a dark, narrow passage or clamber up a steep ladder? Each of us should experience at least once the vexing weirdness of a supposedly homey abode and not just take it for granted. A journey through a house as the exploration of the correlation between inner and outer spaces. The house is different for each — even when it remains the same. "It creates a place that is not a place, an idea of something that we cannot recognize" (Schneider, *Bern Kunsthalle*, 22). We could hardly better express the transformation of the space of de Maistre's soul. Where he was once promised security and an adventure of the soul, now the room traveler is granted only a feeling of insecurity and mental irritation. Schneider's house becomes an artistic emblem of a spatially transcendental rooflessness.

Travel Reading

FOR JOCHEN GERZ

Gerz, Jochen. *Der Transsib.-Prospekt, 1977.* In Jochen Gerz, *Get Out of My Lies.* Wiesbaden, 1997. 84–97. (Also see the review in *Berliner Zeitung* [2000)]: http://www.berlinonline.de/berliner-zeitung/archiv/.bin/dump.fcgi/2000/0404/none/0028/index.html, as well as *Der Spiegel* [1977]: http://wissen.spiegel.de/wissen/dokument/dokument.html?id=40941985&top=SPIEGEL.)

FOR GREGOR SCHNEIDER

Gregor Schneider: Kunsthalle Bern (exhibition catalog). Bern, 1996. (In this there is a long, very instructive interview with Schneider, which later essays often refer to.)

On Schneider's Biennale exhibit: Kittelmann, Udo, ed. *Gregor Schneider: Totes Haus UR; La Biennale di Venezia 2001.* Ostfildern-Ruit, 2001. Also therein: Birnbaum, Daniel. "Vor und nach der Architektur: Unterheydener Straße 12, Rheydt." 63–87.

And his homepage, with numerous links and documents (as well as PDFs of catalogs): http://www.gregorschneider.de/.

Schneider on YouTube: http.//www.youtube.com/watch?v=xMqFSWGBL-c.

Becker, Thorsten. *Mitte.* Berlin, 1994.

Breton, André. *Conversations: The Autobiography of Surrealism.* Trans. Mark Polizzotti. New York, 1993.

Cilauro, Santo, Rob Sitch, and Tom Gleisner. *Molwanien: Land des schadhaften Lächelns.* Trans. Gisbert Haefs. Munich, 2007 (also http://www.amazon.de/Molwanien-schadhaften-L%C3%A4chelns-Santo-Cilauro/dp/3453811380/ref=sr_1_1?ie=UTF8&s=books&qid=1233023098&sr=1-1).

Henry, Joël, Rachael Antony, and Andrew Dean Nystrom. *The Lonely Planet Guide to Experimental Journeys*. Paris, 2005 (also the homepage of LATOUREX: http://www.latourex.org/).

Ici-Même. *Les Paysages étatient extraordinaires*. Grenoble, 2004.

Lubliner, Jean-Paul. *Tour Eiffel: Un Voyage immobile*. Paris, 2000.

Macel, Christine, ed. *Sophie Calle, m'as-tu-vu? Katalog zur Austellung im Centre Pompidou*. November 19, 2003–March 15, 2004. Munich, 2003.

Markowitsch, Rémy. *On Travel*. Nürnberg, 2004.

Ninjalicious (= Jeff Chapman). *Access All Areas: A User's Guide to the Art of Urban Exploration*. Toronto, 2005 (as well as the homepage http://www.infiltration.org/).

Nolan, Christopher, director. *Following*. 69 min. UK, 1998.

Rathenböck, Vera. "Reisen im Wohnzimmer: Die 'Teppiche' der Textilkünstlerin Monika Pichler." *Kulturbericht Oberösterreich* 56. Issue 3/2003. http://www.monikapichler.at/.

Simon, Marie. *Nimm mich mit . . . Eine kleine Geschichte der Reisebegleiter*. Munich, 2005.

http://www.flickr.com/photos/okaitis/sets/72157607423221896/.

http://kalucine.blogspot.com/2007_08_01_archive.html

http://www.myvideo.de/watch/945529/Mein_Zimmer.

http://www.robert.haiss.de/pages/jahre/05_001.html.

Cinematic Explorations

Without going out of my door
I can know all things on Earth

> The Beatles, "The Inner Light"

In order to take a long and distant journey, all one needs
is to cover a little piece of the earth.

> Smolders, *Voyage autour de ma chambre*

How to resist the urge to distance oneself
from the world?

> Smolders, *Voyage autour de ma chambre*

Now and then a song comes along that sings of the distantly near.
And sometimes such a song has a special history that in many ways
is tied to the traveling in place that occurs on a room journey. Such
a thing occurs in a song penned by George Harrison called "The
Inner Light." This Beatles song, which conceives of the room journey as a genuine opening to spiritual experience, appeared in 1968
on the B-side of "Lady Madonna," but first appeared in LP format
on the album *Rarities*. Harrison recorded the audio track in January 1968 in Mumbai, where he composed the music for the film
Wonderwall; its released LP soundtrack was the first solo project
by a Beatle. This film, with Jane Birkin in the starring role, is about

a zoologist who specializes in butterflies, but who one day discovers a hole in the wall of his room through which he can look into the neighboring room. Fascinated, he then gets involved in the (love) life of a photographer and his model, gradually relinquishing any interest in the outside world, and instead remaining interested in his own and particularly the neighbor's room while becoming addicted to the "butterflies in the stomach" of the voyeur. As time goes on, he drills more holes in the wall to better observe the goings-on—always at the risk of being exposed. And at the end, as is so often the case in bad films, what happens is obvious: he saves Penny Lane, which indeed is the name of Jane Birkin's character, who after breaking up with the photographer tries to commit suicide by swallowing pills.

"The Inner Light" was actually not a part of the *Wonderwall* soundtrack, yet it nevertheless takes up the theme of the closed room, nearly raising it to the virtually philosophical. But here the view is directed not toward the adjoining room but rather into the self. For Harrison alludes to chapter 47 of Lao-tzu's *Tao-te Ching*, about which he learned—after a television interview almost entirely about transcendental meditation—from Juan Mascaro, who taught Sanskrit in Cambridge and sent Harrison a copy of his anthology *Lamps of Fire*, in which he highlighted the text from Lao-tzu. What spoke to Harrison was this passage: "Without going out of my door / I can know all things on Earth / Without looking out of my window / I could know the ways of Heaven / The farther one travels / The less one knows / The less one really knows . . . // Arrive without travelling / See all without looking / Do all without doing" (Beatles). Ironically, the full-scale version of the passage was used straightaway by the Beatles in their song "Across the Universe," which takes the space of the room and expands it to the universe. Yet this is also reflected in "The Inner Light": even though it was composed in India, the song proclaims a journey that is possible anywhere by no longer being tied to outer impressions, and yet also takes in the entire world. It's about spiritual experience that is described as a journey, and that in its own way seeks to explore the supposedly familiar world of the self.

In many regards, this theme is also true for various films that in highly different ways attempt to capture room journeys in images. These films, too, depict the journey through a room or into the near-at-hand as a series of images that are often only loosely tied together, most of them relinquishing any kind of clear narrative and instead offering a stream of associated images. Yet in contrast to George Harrison, whose Lao-tzu song enthusiastically embraces the experience of meditation, cinematic room journeys are about loss, nightmares, globalization, or the disappearing sense of any meaning of the human as *sub specie aeternitatis*.

Take for example the recent short film by the Danish artist Ulrik Heltoft, *Voyage autour de ma chambre* (*A Journey around My Room*), from 2008. "Apparently badly wounded and imprisoned in a mysterious room, a man, played by Ulrik Heltoft, inspects his surroundings with an absurd, trance-like attention. He staggers around the room, looks out the tower window, observes the furniture and objects in the room, and finally collapses onto the couch. The room's contours dissolve and are eventually transformed into a hallucinatory experience of the room that eventually leads into a genuinely kaleidoscopic abyss" (Heltoft). The uplifting experience of the near-at-hand is turned on its head into the isolation of a threatening realm that is no longer rooted in a reliable sense of history and feelings attached to objects, but rather mirrors to a greater extent the loss of self.

Raoul Ruiz also had in mind similarly nightmarish images when in a 1984 issue of *Cahiers du cinéma* he published a storyboard of a film in which the room is inside other rooms several times over, and the viewer must discover that he in turn is also being observed. This sketch is in many regards similar to the photo sequence *Things Are Queer* by Duane Michals, who takes up the

19.0, 19.1 Olivier Smolders, *Voyage autour de ma chambre*; film still.

theme of the journey in other ways in order to turn it into a puzzle. To me, Ruiz's film could never work, even if he remained true to the theme of the room in many regards — especially in the filming of Marcel Proust's *In Search of Lost Time*, in which we are indeed given Proust's room, surely the most famous one in world literature, and in which he sat sealed off from outer impressions and wrote his *Recherche*.

Other films, such as Jean Le Gac's *Le Tour du monde*, play with the viewer's imagination, though they never leave the spot from which they depart, in this case Paris — which, as in the era of the *flâneur*, becomes a visual universe: "*A journey through my room?* This film undertakes a tour around the world and yet remains in Paris" (Le Gac). In the era of globalization, we no longer need to travel far away to capture the entire world in images.

This is different from Olivier Smolders's short film *Voyage autour de ma chambre*. "Withdrawing to his room, a cinephile talks about his neighborhood and various journeys, real or imagined, that have affected him or stirred him. From the images gathered over the course of a year, *Voyage autour de ma chambre* explores in

poetic ways the difficulty of finding one's proper place upon the globe." Thus was the film described in the program of the festival where it was shown (and also acclaimed). Even though the images originate from the space of a room, they also stem from many regions of the Earth: from South America, Africa, the Orient, the depths of the oceans; from Florence and other places in Europe. However, these are often made strange with the help of various artistic means. They are somewhat exposed to the effects of the sun, which turn them into strikingly shimmering and bright images that cause the viewer to have to figure out if they are positive or negative. "To lose myself in negative images," Smolders calls it. In this way, they are similar to dream sequences that shimmer and shake, making it hard to recognize what is there, and yet result in a particular visual fascination. As a result, shots that are taken and discarded find a new function in tandem with a room journey that attempts to show all the memories of other journeys as part of one memory.

Furthermore, Smolders differentiated between black-and-white and color images, which can mark the various phases of life: the black-and-white images are mostly memory sequences that

19.2 Olivier Smolders, *Voyage autour de ma chambre*; film still.

make the room journey recognizable as a life journey. "My room lets me think of a place that we don't know and that we cannot picture before life started our heart beating, and about which we can only say something frightening: there we awoke to life. Afterward, we simply walk from room to room, from bed to bed until the last breath. Life now seems a slow progression from one room to another" (Smolders)—or so it says in the film. The room journey thus becomes a cinematic abbreviation for life itself.

However, the traditional color pictures are in turn accompanied by a voice-over that relives the journey through a room in a wider context that globalizes life's journey in another sense: it translates it into a cosmological context. "We live," says the voice-over, "upon a speck of dust that revolves around the sun, which itself is lost among the expanse of the Milky Way. . . . Thus, you and I will return from whence we came, precisely nowhere at all" (Smolders). And Smolders also explores in his images, which range from schools of fish to icebergs, those regions of the globe that appear to be totally absent of any trace of man.

Both spaces, that of memory and the wide-open cosmic space, are associatively tied to each other through objects in the room.

The desk, from which the room journey makes its departure and to which it always returns, is a chamber of wonders *en miniature*: fossils, pieces of agate, and crustaceans in amber are found there next to photographs, reproductions of paintings, and polished cuts of stone, which, with the addition of written symbols in Chinese culture, are transformed into a landscape. Smolders shows in a long series of close-ups these natural forms, which look like landscapes but, as found in nature, take up only a few square centimeters.

The "desire for a place without worries," as it says in the film, finds its fulfillment in the room, but not without taking on a further journey that flows through the body of the room's occupant. When in Florence, Smolders explores along with the camera-snapping tourists the anatomical chamber "La Specola" with long tracking shots; it's for him less about the exposed wax figures from the eighteenth century that reveal cut-open, dissected bodies than it is much more about the experience of the body as a puzzling space, which as a room within a room offers a new journey and also divulges itself to the viewer. It's about the body become image, which in sharp contrast to the tourist opens up a different kind of space that has hardly been explored. "The most uncommon journeys are certainly found in the most unknown regions of our brains. And they are also motionless journeys" (Smolders). Smolders's *Voyage autour de ma chambre* links up with George Harrison's song "The Inner Light" (and also Timm Ulrichs's endoscopic journey through the body) in the designation of the body as a genuine place for a journey—even if it's one that never goes beyond our own four walls.

Travel Reading

The Beatles. "The Inner Light." B-side of the single "Lady Madonna." March 15, 1968, 2:36. Lyrics online at http://oldies.about.com

/gi/dynamic/offsite.htm?zi=1/XJ&sdn=oldies&cdn=entertain
ment&tm=10&f=00&su=p504.1.336.ip_&tt=2&bt=0&bts=1&zu
=http%3A//www.dmbeatles.com/song.php%3Fsong%3D266.

Heltoft, Ulrik. *Voyage autour de ma chambre*, 2008. (Information
about at http://www.kirkhoff.dk.)

Lao-tzu. *Tao-te Ching*. http://www.iging.com/laotse/LaotseD.htm.

Le Gac, Jean. *Le Tour du monde*. Paris, 1975 (book).

————, and Renaud Le Gac. *Le Tour du monde*. 8 min. France, 1982
(film). (Detailed description of the scenario at http://www.cine
matheque.fr/fr/nosactivities/projections/rendez-vous-cine
ma/lecinemadavant-garde/jdp/jeune-dure-pure/chapitre-13
/jean-gac.html.)

Massot, Joe, director. *Wonderwall*. 85 min. UK, 1968.

Michals, Duane. *Things Are Queer*. Exhibition at Fotogalerie Wilde,
Köln, 1972 (also in an "animated" version at http://www.you
tube.com/watch?v=s3XnYOF_CQw).

Ruiz, Raoul. "Story board d'un film en projet: Voyage autour de ma
chambre." *Cahiers du cinéma*, no. 345, March 1983. 55f.

Smolders, Olivier, director. *Voyage autour de ma chambre: Film
immobile*. 26 min. France, 2008. http://www.dailymotion.com
/video/x7jdtt_voyage-autour-de-ma-chambre-olivier_short
films.

Yu, Georges, director. *Voyage autour de ma chambre*. 13 min. Belgium, 1992.

Several websites for room journeys at http://www.myvideo.de
/watch/945529/Mein_Zimmer.

TWENTIETH LEG

Near Distance

I will write the *On the Road* for my generation.
It will be called *Stay Home*.

> Green, back cover

In the countryside of "Vue des Alpes" we are tourists — little
beings with big eyes. Our rambling gaze doesn't help us to look
too deeply into things, for we are flâneurs, not discoverers.

> Storz, no page

A dream comes true: finally, there is a vacation available to
everyone, and completely free to boot. All it requires is a visit to
the website of a family called M. and Ch. Studer van den Berg, alias
Monica Studer and Christoph van den Berg, and there reserve a
room. However, this unusual hotel has been booked solid for some
time. And for those who wait for an opening, it comes as no surprise at all. What's offered is a mountain landscape some 1,600
meters high, as described in the books, with the possibility of es-
caping into a superb, remote mountainous area of some 20 square
kilometers, with trails for hiking and climbing, even a lake that
is 43 meters deep and on which one can make little excursions
with a paddleboat, as well as a mountain railway with fantastic
views. The region is hardly known by other tourists, such that the
walking paths can often be used completely undisturbed. In addi-

20.0 Monica Studer and Christoph van den Berg, *Vue des Alpes*; in Monica Studer, Christoph van den Berg, and Andreas Baur, eds., *Being a Guest* (Basel, 2003), 10.

tion, there is even one of those impressive glaciers that elsewhere threaten to disappear. The climate is moderate (for the most part a comfortable room temperature) and the sun really shines all the time, which even nowadays in summer is not at all the norm. The vacationer can rent a 13.5-square-meter, tastefully appointed and comfortable single or double room with a terrace that guarantees an unobstructed view of the mountains, is easy to get to, and also has the advantage of offering environmentally friendly tourism — because this hotel exists only on the Internet.

And yet a reservation is essential, because only by making one will the traveler be able to book a room; otherwise it, like other parts of the hotel, will not be available. It is thus an actual hotel, in which there are guests, and which respects their privacy. The visitor is always free to hike through the mountainous countryside, to clamber up the path to the mountain hut, to take a look through the guest book and thus get a taste of a later visit. On the Internet, there is also a prospectus with the most important information and enticing offers: "How would you like to spend a relaxing week in the Alps while staying at home and finishing off all the work that otherwise would be left undone? Why not get away from it all without neglecting your daily chores? Haven't you had enough of congested motorways and overbooked flights during the holiday season? Since summer 2001 the Vue des Alpes project gives you the opportunity to make a reservation for a digital stay of five consecutive days in a fictional room in our exclusively rendered spa hotel, situated in a stimulating, computer-generated scenery. No traffic noise, no hordes of boisterous, fun seeking package-holiday makers will disturb you in your mountainous seclusion! On this site you will book one of nine cozily furnished double rooms (equipped with 3D comfort, view guaranteed in all rooms), on arrival you will be given a code for your room and during your stay you can enjoy the full comfort of the hotel as often as you please" (vuedesalpes.com).

What's being offered? Indeed, the hotel leaves hardly any wish left unfulfilled, as the list of touristic possibilities shows on the homepage:

Walks in the unique 3D alpine scenery done in Riven/Myst style
Full board
Illustrious guests (you can check the bookings in our guest book at
    any time)
Pedal boat trips on the lake
Unlimited free rides on the Gleissenhorn aerial railway
Beautiful souvenirs at customer-friendly prices
CD-rom of your stay produced in our in-house photo studio
Evening entertainment with the duo "Moni and Chris"

What more could one want? I've already made a reservation, though unfortunately I have to wait a year to take my vacation.*
Monica Studer and Christoph van den Berg's artistic project

---

* PS (almost a year after the writing of this chapter): this vacation finally took place (right at the end of the semester) — and it didn't disappoint!

20.1 Monica Studer and Christoph van den Berg, *Vue des Alpes*; in Monica Studer, Christoph van den Berg, and Andreas Baur, eds., *Being a Guest* (Basel, 2003), 11.

20.2 Vue des Alpes; website screen shot.

plays with the lure of the Internet, which we already know how to navigate, and which allows us to continually travel, and for which the countless number of webcams makes possible virtual journeys in real time. In the tourist industry, the formula of the "virtual journey" has already made the rounds, which the Swiss artists ironically point out. Their hotel project offers a means of traveling in place amid the swift navigation of hundreds of websites, which we now usually visit just for a short while before leaving. In a booked room, we can take a vacation from restless travel on the Internet and wander through the peace of a countryside that almost archetypically imitates the Swiss mountain region without providing a concrete model. Nor does this hotel vacation offer a journey through photographs of acquaintances, but rather through its own constructed virtual world, which visitors in effect distinguish from those they are more familiar with, realizing that it does not promise, like *Second Life* or *World of Warcraft*, new encounters, suspense, mystery, and thrills, but instead just restorative peace and quiet: "Vue des Alpes is no adventure game. There are no puzzles to be solved with a mouse click, no monsters to be killed, no treasures to be raised. There is just the idyll of fresh and clean air in the mountains." During your visit, you can also send your friends postcards with views of the countryside. The Sacri Monti, which we encountered on the Second Leg, have been transformed into virtual mountains, which are also meant to supersede what was formerly an exhausting journey.

Also, visitors who are always expecting a chat room in any room on the Internet will find no such thing here: "In case you are looking to chat with digital vacationers or to flirt with someone while on vacation, you've definitely got the wrong address: Hotel Vue des Alpes is not a graphic chat room. This is for your information so that you won't be disappointed when you don't meet up with anyone during your visit. Consider Vue des Alpes as the place on the Internet where you are not forced to have to continually commune with others."

This was exactly the idea of what the Internet would be in the era of media theory in general. Such visions — willingly or unwillingly, since they were actually utopian — were disproportionately gloomy. Vilém Flusser titled a chapter of his book *Ins Universum der technischen Bilder* (*Into the Universe of Technical Images*) "Kammermusik" ("Room Music"), and in doing so not only struck music's thematic strings but also touched on room journeys. In this chapter there is a "fable," a vision of the telematic human being of the future: "People will sit in separate cells, playing with their fingertips on keyboards, staring at tiny screens, receiving, changing, and sending images. . . . People will be in contact with one another through their fingertips, and so form a dialogical net, a global super-brain. . . . A universal spectacle, . . . it will be a mosaic spectacle, a game with tiny pieces, . . . a black box composed entirely of many darkened rooms, a universal orchestra of numerous chamber musicians" (Flusser 161–62). The Internet was imagined as a network of dark chambers that would communicate with one another in multiple ways and make travel superfluous, the lure of the distant in fact long since falling behind the endless widening of the near distance of the Internet.

The distant draws nearer. This is according to the analysis of Edith Decker and Peter Weibel, who more than twenty years ago took stock of the relationships between telecommunications and art. The possibilities already suggested by telecommunications in their time led to "zero journeys," to the "substitution of home for the world" (Decker and Weibel 47). Acceleration is the rule and the point, the room the place in which the mad dash comes to a standstill. The room journey is the focal point, as well as the new technical media and secondary forms of communication. "The immobility of the body, of the subject, is in opposition to the dynamism and speed of images and symbols. People no longer wish to travel, and when they travel, they don't want to see anything. Because images now travel to them" (Decker and Weibel 48).

* * *

Paul Verhoeven's film *Total Recall* (much like David Cronenberg's *eXistence* and the *Matrix* trilogy from the Wachowski brothers) transformed this vision into a story about a journey into images. Douglas Quaid (Arnold Schwarzenegger), a construction worker who lives a totally unremarkable life, tries to play out his dreams of an exciting life in earnest in the form of a thrilling journey to Mars, thereby getting mixed up with the agency REKALL, Inc., which promises to plant virtual memories inside him that will nevertheless provide the same sensory qualities as real memories. In this nether zone between the real and the virtual, he soon finds himself caught up in a very abstruse spy story about nothing less than the liberation of Mars, which indeed succeeds, though it remains unclear if it is real or virtual. "What if this is all a dream?" Quaid therefore asks his new girlfriend, the rebellious Melina, at the end of the film. She responds with the only answer there is: "Kiss me quick before you wake up."

Travel Reading

ON STUDER AND VAN DEN BERG'S *VUE DES ALPES-PROJECT*

http://www.vuedesalpes.com/home_d.html.

Storz, Reinhard. "Your Visit to the Hotel Vue des Alpes." http://www.vuedesalpes.com/home_d.html.

Studer, Monica, Christoph van den Berg, and Andreas Baur, eds. *Being a Guest*. Basel, 2003.

Vögele, Christoph, ed. *Somewhere Else Is the Same Place* (exhibition catalog, Kunstmuseum Solothurn). Zürich, 2005.

Wüllner, Jo. *Über das Reisen in wahre Wirklichkeiten*. http://www.argentario-almanacco.it/601_Turismo/601_de.html.

Decker, Edith, and Peter Weibel, eds. *Vom Verschwinden der Ferne: Telekommunikation und Kunst*. Köln, 1990.

Flusser, Vilém. *Into the Universe of Technical Images*. Trans. Nancy Ann Roth. Minneapolis, London, 2011.

Green, Adam. *magazine*. Frankfurt am Main, 2005.

Verhoeven, Paul, director. *Total Recall*. 115 min. USA, 1990.

The Final Journey

Travel means getting accustomed to death.

Houssaye, 230

And so perhaps we are also on the path of the great journey.

Letter of Xavier de Maistre to his niece Adèle de Maistre, April
25, 1839 (de Maistre, 182)

Not to live life in its truest way is a crime, not just against
oneself, but against others as well.

Cortázar and Dunlop, 37

Certainly the most touching brief journey, namely Carol Dunlop
and Julio Cortázar's *Die Autonauten auf der Kosmobahn* (*Autonauts
of the Cosmoroute*), presents itself in the tradition of the surrealist
journey, and above all is a wonderful love story. In 1982, the two of
them undertake a "quite surreal 'expedition'" (Cortázar and Dunlop 15) along a stretch of road that could not be more ordinary:
the highway from Paris to Marseille. Both know as they head out
that they will soon die, each being already stricken with terminal illness. Dunlop will not live to see the publication of the book.
Cortázar dedicates a postscript to her in which death becomes the
"solitary journey" (Cortázar and Dunlop 353) and the highway a
metaphor of their life together, which continues. *Autonauts of the*

Cosmoroute not only takes up the classical motif of death as the last journey and transforms it into a love story and the utopia of a worthwhile life. The couple's trip on the highway, which recently was the subject of the film *Lucie et maintenant* (*Lucia and Now*), is also an alternative form of the road movie of contemporary film in its link with death—although numerous other films of the genre, such as *Thelma and Louise*, *Death Proof*, and *Natural Born Killers*, also culminate in death or the traveler's road being paved with corpses. Dunlop and Cortázar's journey, in contrast, offers the peaceful exploration of a "closed microcosm" (Cortázar and Dunlop 57) through which the world is transformed as if by magic. Their van becomes the gentle dragon Fafner, Dunlop and Cortázar a Little Bear and Wolf, and the highway a paradise.

In driving from Paris to Marseille on the "highway of the sun," which even with traffic jams and heavy traffic can be accomplished in a few hours, Dunlop and Cortázar plan to break up the journey in particular ways. They will stop at each rest area along the way and spend the night there. Because time runs short, they have to abandon this project, but indeed the journey that they actually took, which lasted thirty-two days, from May 23 to June 23, 1982, follows these guidelines for the most part. Here, then, are the rules:

1. Complete the journey from Paris to Marseille without once leaving the autoroute.
2. Explore each one of the rest areas, at the rate of two per day, spending the night in the second one without exception.
3. Carry out scientific topographical studies of each rest area, taking note of all pertinent observations.
4. Taking our inspiration from the travel tales of the great explorers of the past, write the book of the expedition (methods to be determined). (Cortázar and Dunlop 33)

DIE EXPEDITION

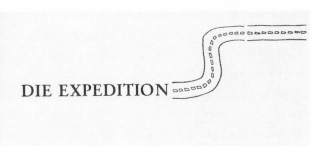

Der feierliche, wenngleich etwas chaotische Augenblick des Aufbruchs der Expedition. Freunde und Helfer schreiten zu den letzten Kontrollen.

21.0 Departure; in Julio Cortázar and Carol Dunlop, *Autonauts of the Cosmoroute: Eine zeitlose Reise Paris-Marseille* (Frankfurt am Main, 1996), 47.

The journey is planned as a formal expedition—with a comprehensive list of supply stations for taking on provisions (some included for their health needs); a carefully prepared set of travel accounts ranging from James Cook, who is often quoted in room journeys, to Jean Charcot's account of his South Pole expedition (also regularly quoted from); and not least of all a precise documentation of the journey in words and images, presented as a scientific text complete with notes, and bearing many of the features of ethnological journals. Cortázar and Dunlop note with ironic distance the "indigenous customs" (Cortázar and Dunlop 130) of the natives; make detailed sketches of the rest areas that are usually stereotypical, though coded to a particular region; and also observe the effects of globalization at the rest stops where various types of souvenirs made in China are for sale.

But why in fact the highway? There could hardly be a road any less attractive, any more monotonous. Yet the highway is the architectural symbol of acceleration in "this century of obligatory speed" (Cortázar and Dunlop 25). The chosen stretch of road—as anyone who has driven it will remember—could therefore reliably be covered in a specific amount of time. The time of entry and departure is marked precisely at each toll plaza. And the highway is "not just this ribbon of asphalt laid out for speed, punctuated by utilitarian and hygienic stops" (Cortázar and Dunlop 32), which serves to influence the driver's behavior and reflexes, according to the text; it also merges into "that great impersonal totality so sought after by religions" (Cortázar and Dunlop 24). It is an expression of the organized mobility by which the modern defines itself. It is an emblem of instrumental rationality, of "normalization" and of acceleration as a basic condition of the modern.

Hartmut Rosa has set forth a theory of modernization based on the phenomenon of acceleration. His theory starts from the central observation that the modern is distinguished by a social and technological acceleration that threatens to lead to its opposite:

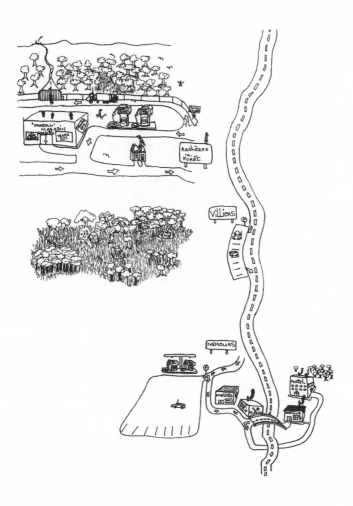

21.1 Sketch; in Julio Cortázar and Carol Dunlop, *Autonauts of the Cosmoroute: Eine zeitlose Reise Paris-Marseille* (Frankfurt am Main, 1996), 63.

Der Garten der Versuchung mit einer verschlüsselten Botschaft (blauer Lappen). Glaubte die Gesellschaft, daß wir voller Verzweiflung in die Fluchtfalle gehen würden?

21.2   Garden of temptation; in Julio Cortázar and Carol Dunlop, *Autonauts of the Cosmoroute: Eine zeitlose Reise Paris-Marseille* (Frankfurt am Main, 1996), 88.

"a far-reaching structural and cultural shutdown, a historical rigidity, in which *nothing essentially* changes despite rapid transformations on the surface" (Rosa 16). Rosa thinks of his critical reconstruction of social acceleration as a contribution to a "yet-to-be-written sociology of the good life, . . . which will take a critical stance against the structural conditions of a society dominated by implicit and explicit *concepts of the successful life*." These not only inform the implicit normativization of the structures of time but also lead quite often to esoteric concepts that contrast acceleration with a *different* kind of time.

Julio Cortázar and Carol Dunlop's decelerated journey seeks precisely to fulfill the concept of a "successful life" without falling into escapism. "This expedition is not at all escapist" (Cortázar and

Wissenschaftliche Arbeitsanordnung im Innern Fafnirs.

21.3 Materials for gathering scientific observations; in Julio Cortázar and Carol Dunlop, *Autonauts of the Cosmoroute: Eine zeitlose Reise Paris-Marseille* (Frankfurt am Main, 1996), 334.

Dunlop 108), they note, nor do they take on an antimodernization attitude at any point. In the complex constellation of acceleration and deceleration — and not just because of the speed of the passing cars — they discover a "parallel highway" (Cortázar and Dunlop 48, 120) that at least for a while appears to them like a paradise. An excerpt from their travel account takes up the paradise metaphor explicitly and applies it to the highway rest stop called "Parkingland" (Cortázar and Dunlop 126), an "emptiness with décor" (Cortázar and Dunlop 132), which is always the same and yet is a "world of liberty" (Cortázar and Dunlop 126). Ironically, this Parkingland paradise is enclosed by a chain-link fence and suggests a microcosm of the highway rest stop, in which they, like Xavier de Maistre, make discovery after discovery. The rest stop as a "rest area" becomes a "presence full of life and riches" (Cortázar and Dunlop

91). And even more emphatically: "The rest areas are the place and time of truth" (Cortázar and Dunlop 92).

This truth, this *successful life*, is found not only in the discovery of "a life that can only be defined as *natural*" (Cortázar and Dunlop 103) and the attempt "to live life in its truest way" (Cortázar and Dunlop 41), but also above all in transformation through love. That is the successful life — nothing more, but also nothing less: "The freeway is me, you, us, and when your tongue looks for mine and unwinds. . . . We won't leave the autoroute in Marseille, my love, dearest, or anywhere else" (Cortázar and Dunlop 283 ff.). This journey is the discovery of "our happiness in full technological clamour, which lovingly obliterated us" (Cortázar and Dunlop 19). As for the "pale and intrepid reader" and the "companion of these pages," they hope — and this wish also goes out to the reader of the present book — to have "opened some doors for you too," hoping "that some parallel freeway project of your own invention is already germinating" (Cortázar and Dunlop 37).

Travel Reading

Caillot, Antoine. *Voyage religieux et sentimental aux quatres cimetières de Paris*. Paris, 1809.

Cortázar, Julio, and Carol Dunlop. *Autonauts of the Cosmoroute*. Trans. Anne McLean. Brooklyn, 2007.

Fürbringer, Simone, Nicolas Humbert, and Werner Penzel, directors. *Lucie et maintenant: Journal nomade*. 86 min. Germany, 2007.

Houssaye, Arsène. "Voyage à Venise." In Houssaye, *Œuvres*, vol. 4. Paris, 1855.

Maistre, Xavier de. *Lettres à sa famille*. Ed. Gabriel de Maistre. 3 vols. Vol. 3. Clermond-Ferrand, 2006.

Rosa, Hartmut. *Beschleunigung: Die Veränderung der Zeitstruktur in der Moderne*. Frankfurt am Main, 2006.

Acknowledgments

The long journey through the history of room travel would not have been possible without a wide array of support and numerous travel companions.

I wish to thank the Fondation Maison des Sciences de l'Homme in Paris, and particularly Hinnerk Bruhns, for the invitation to work there as a visiting scholar, which allowed me to track down a number of hard-to-find texts from French literature.

My deep thanks also to Christine Klessinger of the Hotel Olympic in Munich for the chance to present the project in a place for which it was made.

For advice, inspiration, and various support, I'd also like to thank Nicolas Berg, Fritz Breithaupt, Petra Büscher, Thomas Fechner-Smarsly, Christiane Heibach, Klaus Kufeld, Felix Lentz, Dieter Martin, Dominique Miollan, Karoline Müller-Stahl, Joachim Paech, Annegret Pelz, Willem van Reijen, François Rey, Alexander Roesler, Robert Stockhammer, Juliane Vogel, Martin Weinmann, David Wellbery, and Elisabeth and Jürgen Wolf, as well as both seminars in Mannheim and Konstanz where the first selection of texts was discussed.

My special and heartfelt thanks go to Lea Heim, Annie Hofmann (also for the translation of numerous French quotations), Ingeborg Moosmann, Alexander Müller, Morten Paul, and Kathrin Schönegg, without whom the journey of this book through texts and images would have remained mere wandering.

Translator's Note

The original text on which the translation is based is titled *Reisender Stillstand: Eine kleine Kulturgeschichte der Reisen im und um das Zimmer herum* (Frankfurt am Main: S. Fischer Verlag, 2010).

For various texts quoted by the author that have been translated into English, I have used available English translations, then listed them as such in the "Travel Reading" section at the end of each leg of the journey. For those texts that are not quoted but instead cited as general reference, I have supplied the bibliographic citation found in the German text of the "Travel Reading." All other quoted texts are translated by me from the German versions found in the original.

I wish to thank the Geisteswissenschaften International for funding the translation, and Barbara Perlmutter for her help in finding a publisher. I am also grateful to Susan Bielstein and Anthony Burton for their editorial support and guidance. My thanks also to Bernd Stiegler for his patient help in answering a number of queries along the way, and for his good company on the journey of this translation.

Index of Names

Harrison, George, 221–23, 227
Hauser, Heinrich, 161
Heilborn, Adolf, 62, 65, 81, 87f.
Heller, Stephen, 15
Heltoft, Ulrik, 223, 228
Henriot, Emile, 185
Henry, Joël, 220
Hermann, Bernard, 109–11
Hessel, Franz, 89, 125, 128–31
Hetzel, Pierre-Jules (pseud. P. J. Stahl),
  91–93, 95f., 98–100
Hoer, C., 103f.
Hoffmann, Ernst Theodor Amadeus, 58,
  65, 124
Holmes, Oliver Wendell, 103f., 111
Hong, Edna H., 121
Hong, Howard N., 121
Houssaye, Arsène, 42, 50, 53, 58–63, 65,
  123f., 131, 237, 244
Howard, Richard, 193
Howe, John, 178
Hughes, Howard, 160f.
Hühnchen, Leberecht, 113f., 121
Humbert, Nicolas, 244
Hurley, Andrew, 192
Huysmans, Joris-Karl, 137, 139–42, 144,
  146–48

Ibrahim, Kamal, 185, 188, 193
Innocent VIII, pope, 18

Jacob, Hans, 148
Jamin, Jean, 162
Jaquet, Friedrich David, 5, 7, 16, 41, 50
Jennings, Michael, 80
Jephcott, Edmund, 170
Johannot, Tony, 62, 91, 93–100
Jourdan, J. L. E. B., 48, 50, 81, 89
Jung, Jörg, 215–17
Jung, Ralf Raimo, 215–17
Jünger, Ernst, 150

Kant, Immanuel, 15, 34
Karr, Alphonse, 39, 50, 54, 67, 69, 72–
  76, 80
Kerbellec, Philippe G., 150, 161
Kersting, Georg Friedrich, 35
Kierkegaard, Sören, 113, 116–21
Kilic, Ilse, 188, 193

Kittelmann, Udo, 216, 219
Klopstock, Friedrich Wilhelm, 93
Knight, Thomas Andrew, 71
Kohlmaier, Georg, 77f.
Köhn, Eckhardt, 125, 130, 132
Kracauer, Siegfried, 164f., 170
Kramer, Fritz, 172, 179
Kretschmann, Karl Friedrich, 62, 65
Krull, Germaine, 127

La Liborlière, Louis-François-Marie
  Bellin de, 83–85, 89
La Roche, Sophie von, 29–35, 37
Labiche, Eugène, 16
Landgraf, Gabriele, 19, 27
Lang, Jack, 212
Langen, August, 65
Lao-tzu, 222f., 228
Lapeyrousse, Jean François Galaup, 107
Lavers, Annette, 138
Le Gac, Jean, 224, 228
Le Gac, Renaud, 228
Leibniz, Gottfried Wilhelm, 195
Leiris, Michel, 150, 156–60, 162
Lessing, Gotthold Ephraim, 29, 34
Leuwers, Daniel, 15f., 156, 162
Lévi-Strauss, Claude, 171f., 179, 209
Lexa and Wild, 104
Linden, Adrien, 50
Livingstone, Rodney, 131, 170
Loster-Schneider, Gudrun, 32–34, 37
Lotringer, Sylvère, 163, 170
Lubliner, Jean-Paul, 211–14, 220

Macel, Christine, 220
Maeterlinck, Maurice, 196
Magellan, Ferdinand de, 9
Maintenon, Françoise d'Aubigné, 34
Maistre, Adèle de, 237
Maistre, Gabriel de, 16, 27, 102, 111
Maistre, Joseph de, 7f., 16
Maistre, Xavier de, 2, 4, 7–16, 39, 41, 43,
  47f., 53f., 63f., 94, 101f., 111, 123–25,
  128f., 181–84, 190, 192f., 206f., 210,
  218, 237, 243f.
Mangin, Arthur, 40, 43–47, 50
Mansour, Joyce, 193
Markowitsch, Rémy, 209, 220
Mascaro, Juan, 222